A Guide to Self-Mastery

Change Your Life by
Changing Your Thoughts
Through the Law of Attraction,
Master Key System,
Mindfulness,
Meditation and
Visualization

Tammy Gallagher

I

TAMGALL
PUBLISHING

Contents

A FREE GIFT FOR OUR READERS

Get my free eBook on sweeteners...the good, the bad and the ugly. Which sweeteners to avoid and which provide health benefits.

Visit *www.tamgall.com/sweeteners-ebook*

Author's Preface

Imagine for a moment that your perspective is just an inkling of the accurate makeup of the truth. Imagine you have unlimited resources and the power to create anything and everything you desire. Imagine that you control every situation or circumstance in your life, and nothing is beyond your control.

Now stop imagining… and believe!

This is a factual truth and the potential you have been empowered with. This is, in effect, what has created your reality and will continue to create your reality.

What is it that you want out of life? Health, love, money? You can have all these things. The world often refers to this process as the *Law of Attraction*. You must train your mind to create the proper thoughts and visions, and the seed of thought will be planted and grow into a belief that will ultimately deliver to you the circumstance consistent with your heart's desires. It sounds simple. Well, here's the story...

Scientists often state that we use only about ten percent of our brain's capacity. Have you ever wondered what you could achieve using one hundred percent of your brain's ability? Many consider *The Master Key System*, written by Charles F. Haanel, the key to opening that door.

Haanel wrote several books published by Psychology Publishing and his Master Key Institute. In addition to *The Master Key System*, which he wrote in 1912, he also wrote *Mental Chemistry* and *The New Psychology*.[1]

By 1933, *The Master Key System* had sold more than 200,000 copies and seemingly vanished. It resurfaced many years later.[1] This system teaches the ultimate principles, causes, effects, and laws that bring about all achievement and success. It is said that *The Master Key System* shows you how to get what you want in life. My experience with *The Master Key System* has been amazing!

In November 2006, I began studying with a good friend. If I recall correctly, this is about when the documentary, *The Secret,* came out. We had a weekly master mind meeting, during which we explored universal laws and related them to our beliefs. It was at this time that we began to study the *Master Key*.

Although *The Master Key System* seemed profound and impactful, it was a challenging read and outdated. Not only did it need to be updated with current terminology, but life has progressed since the early 1900s, and much of what was written was challenging to relate to. Despite these things, I continued to review the first two lessons repeatedly. Something inside me told me I needed to go through all twenty-four lessons. I was inspired to begin re-writing each lesson in my own words in simple, easy-to-read terminology that applied to today's world. By doing this, I not only created *The Guide to Self-Mastery* but also was able to plant the seeds of thought that grew into an unconscious understanding of the teachings.

I found that changing the way I thought and prayed allowed me to realize the extent to which God is within me and how He wants me to succeed more than I can imagine. This new way of using my mental power allowed me to expand my mind and feel more in sync with God and the Universe in ways I never thought possible.

This information will open your mind and allow you to realize the unlimited possibilities that are within your reach, and how to use your connection with Eternal Energy to construct the life you've always wanted.

The Master Key System sets out the fundamental principles of life and creative living as Haanel understood and applied them. *The Guide to Self Mastery* is my interpretation of Charles Haanel's original writings. Essential to his teaching is the proper development and use of mental power – the key to genuinely creative power and action, harmony and health, love and happiness, and abundant possibilities.

To effectively integrate the teachings of *The Guide to Self-Mastery* into your life, it is essential that you commit to three to five months of study and practice. There are no shortcuts here. Reading *The Guide to Self-Mastery* like a novel from cover to cover will give you some benefits, but to transform your life and make your new way of thinking an unconscious habit, make the three to five-month commitment. It will only take about thirty minutes each day, and the reward will be significant.

Each chapter represents four to seven days of study. You must read, re-read and listen to each chapter multiple times and complete the appropriate chapter meditation exercises consistently and regularly during the four to seven days to master each lesson. You move on to the next chapter and meditation exercise when you strongly understand the prior chapter material and have mastered the chapter exercise.

In this book, I refer to God in many ways. The Infinite, the Divine, and the All-Powerful are just a few. God's spirit I refer to also in alternate ways, such as Universal Energy and Eternal Energy. God's intelligence and resources I often refer to as the Universal Mind. Ultimately, I believe in God. And if you believe in a higher power, a Creator, then feel free to substitute your beliefs within the scope of this book. My intention here is not to teach any religion but instead to teach universal laws, and it is up to you to put it into the context of your religion.

You are about to transform yourself, and it is a journey that will revolutionize how you think and renovate your core beliefs. Each step of the process prepares you for the next.

> *"... (it) is like driving at night in the fog. You can only see as far as your headlights, but you can make the whole trip that way."*
>
> ~Edgar Lawrence Doctorow, Author

Embrace each week and focus on the study and meditation exercise within that week alone, and the transformation will unfold effortlessly. You'll be given step by step instructions to learn mindfulness, meditation, creative visualization, and more.

You are about to start a journey to explore the power of the Divine within you, integrate your understanding of Supreme Law, master the *Law of Attraction*, and connect with the Universal Mind. You are about to start a journey that will change your life!

Introduction

It was December 26, 1989, the day I had hoped would be the happiest day of my life. I was getting married. I had dated my fiancé for only about six months, and my inner voice was telling me that I was rushing into this, but he kept moving up the date and had a sense of urgency that was unexplainable to me. Ignoring my gut feeling, I got married on that day.

Everything happened so quickly. We bought a home in January, and I was blessed and conceived in February.

As newlyweds, we needed things for our new home, we went on a beautiful honeymoon, and in addition to other things, we promptly accumulated debt. Between the two of us, I was the one with good credit, so this debt was in my name.

As quickly as all of this occurred, just as quickly it all fell apart. We were separated after only four months of marriage and divorced shortly after that. Soon to become a single mother, I changed jobs because I regularly traveled, which would quickly be out of the question.

In addition to becoming pregnant, separating, divorcing, and changing jobs to a commissioned position, I had another battle to fight. All the debt we had accumulated was in my name, including my wedding ring, which I later found out, and my now ex-husband was not taking responsibility for any of it. I had less than $100 to my name, and I couldn't see the light at the end of the tunnel. I did what I had never before imagined I would do and filed for bankruptcy.

Shortly after my son was born, he required an operation. It was a routine operation common in boys; however, this $14,000 operation was not within my finances. The court order requiring the father to carry medical insurance was ignored, as the father canceled my son's medical insurance. Add this to the significant amount of unpaid child support and the fact that the father moved away and hadn't seen his son since shortly after his birth; I decided it would be better if I controlled our destiny. I returned to court and gained full custody of my son.

My life was turned upside down, inside out, and somehow, someway, it was the best thing that had ever happened to me!

Let me explain...

During this process, I never once thought about aborting my son. I believed that he was meant for greatness. Why else would he have been given to me so quickly? Me...the one who couldn't possibly consider giving up a child. It was as if God knew that this soul was meant to be born, and that's why I had been chosen to be the mother.

Additionally, the thought that raising a child on my own would be difficult had never occurred to me. It didn't matter that my family wasn't local, and I didn't have much support. I knew I'd somehow be given what I needed when needed.

As a result of what most would consider a nightmare, not only was I blessed with an awesome son, but I found a career that was meant for me: a business that I love, that I'm good at, and that compensates well. When I was 'forced' to find another job, I took a position as a new home sales associate. Seventeen years later, I progressed from novice sales associate with no college degree to division president.

I ran a multimillion-dollar division of the world's most experienced home builder.

The entire journey was one of amazement when I looked back. For example, one of the minimum requirements of most positions I held since 1995 was a bachelor's degree in business or a related field. I didn't even complete my associate degree, much less a bachelor's.

Additionally, men predominantly run residential development due to the work involved. Not many women are in construction and development compared to men. Not only do I not have a degree, but upon my departure, I was the only female division president nationwide for this builder. What a fantastic experience and accomplishment that I never could have imagined!

Fast forward to 2015, and although there was much in between, the final position I held was senior vice president over a region of seven divisions. I don't share this with you to impress you, but to impress upon you that belief creates impressive results. This want ad for a new home salesperson with no experience needed appearing in front of me in 1990 ultimately led me to a 28-year career.

In the mid-1990s, when my career began to kick in high gear, I believed that much of what was occurring to me was good luck. I used to say that life planned my career better than I could have planned it myself.

I now know that I planned all of it. In 1990, when I first began to understand that my marriage wasn't going to last, I attached myself to the book *The Official Guide to Success* by Tom Hopkins. I was convinced that Hopkin's material, when applied, could significantly improve my results.

The Official Guide to Success became my 'sanity bible.' I learned, among other things, that if I 'faked it,' I'd make it.[2] It would all work out if I pretended to be the person I desired to be. It would only be a matter of time before I became that person. Anything, and everything, I could do to keep the fear, doubt, and worry out of my mind I did. And this book helped me tremendously.

I had a theme song that I sang whenever I began to feel down and felt like I was sliding into depression. Somehow, as I began to sing this uplifting song, it would bring me back to a happier state.

I additionally sang *You Are My Sunshine* to my son while rocking him to sleep. I knew he was such a blessing, and it would all work out if I stayed focused on my blessings.

The Official Guide to Success was the first book I read that focused on the power of positive thinking, the power within. This book proved to me that there is power in our thoughts. This is the book that started me on my journey that led to *A Guide to Self-Mastery*.

Instructions

Chapter Material

Most people will want to read this book like a novel, and although you may decide to do so, I suggest afterwards, you re-read the book in the following format.

There are five activities listed below, and I recommend that you complete every activity with each chapter before progressing to the next chapter. I also suggest that you complete a minimum of one activity per day and all five activities within the four-to-seven-day period for each lesson chapter.

- Read the chapter silently

- Read the chapter aloud

- Listen to the audio of the chapter

- Listen to the audio of the chapter while simultaneously silently reading the chapter

- Listen to the audio of the chapter while highlighting in the book or taking notes on the impactful messages

Exercises

Each chapter has a meditation exercise. It would be best if you invest fifteen to thirty minutes per day. All the meditation exercises will require you to select a room where you can be alone and undisturbed. This should be a place that is accessible daily. You'll be asked to sit erectly in a chair or on the ground, or lie on your back in your bed or on the ground or a mat. Select your room based on what's appropriate for your preferred position and one that will be available for a minimum of three to five months for the twenty-four-chapter lessons.

The first four exercises will ultimately bring you through the steps to meditation. Others describe this process as preparing yourself to receive the Holy Spirit in prayer. These exercises may be a refresher if you're used to meditating or praying in silence with only controlled thought.

Exercises five through twenty-four should start by bringing yourself to this meditative state. It is in meditation, when you inhibit uncontrolled thoughts and have control over your body and mind, where you connect with the Divine.

All exercises ask you to sit erect or lie comfortably on your back without lounging. If you're lying down, keep your feet apart about shoulder width or slightly closer with your feet comfortably open to the outside. Keep your hands at your sides with your palms down, or place one on your stomach and one on your heart. Your head and neck should be in alignment with your spine so that your spine through your head is level.

If you're sitting and are used to meditating, you may take your traditional meditative position. Otherwise, it is suggested that you sit comfortably on the floor with your legs crossed Indian style. If you prefer to sit on a chair, do so erectly with your feet flat on the floor. Do not cross your legs. In either case, place your hands on your legs or knees comfortably with your palms down. While sitting, you can also bring your hands together if you prefer. Again, you want to keep your spine aligned with your neck and head.

Keeping your spine, neck, and head aligned allows for the most direct physical connection between your brain and gut. Your second brain is located in the gut. The gut-brain, known as the enteric nervous system, is a mass of nerves embedded in the walls of our gastrointestinal tract, most of which reside in the midsection or the gut.

The enteric nervous system can operate independently of the brain, which is why it's referred to as our second brain.[3] The vagus nerve connects the two brains, which is how they communicate. It's also believed that gut health can directly affect our mental health.[4] The phrase 'gut feeling' has some science to back it up.

Why is it essential to sit erect and keep the head, neck, and spine in alignment during meditation? Most will say that it helps with deep breathing, but from my experience, I'm convinced that this communication between both brains is enhanced and makes meditation more impactful.

Once you have identified the location and the physical position you intend to take during the meditation exercises, you must also ensure the proper environment. Do not have any noise in the background, with the exception of mellow instrumental music, if you prefer. Turn cellular phones off and any other items that could cause an interruption.

This is the environment, location, and position you will duplicate for every meditation exercise. Therefore, be sure to choose a room and position that will be appropriate and comfortable for all the meditations for up to twenty-four weeks and beyond.

Each meditation must be repeated six times before moving to the next chapter. You can complete the meditation exercise once or twice per day and continue the meditation until you have it mastered. You may progress to the next chapter only after learning the meditation exercise and developing a solid understanding of the chapter content. If completed correctly, this should take four to seven days per chapter.

Let's get started.

All Power Comes from Within

Chapter One

Do you ever notice that everything goes your way when you get on a roll? Or that the people who have everything seem to get even more? It's as if the wealthy get wealthier and the poor get poorer. The healthy never have to worry about their health, and the sick get sicker. What about those people who never seem to get a break?

Ultimately, we tend to get more of whatever we have going on in our lives, whether we like it or not. Why is this so? That's what we are going to explore, and if you understand this, then you should be able to change it at will, wouldn't you think?

Your reality is a reflection of your beliefs, and your beliefs are shaped by your conscious thought interpreting what you observe every day.

Suppose you knew failure wasn't possible and success was already guaranteed, that you had all the power of the most powerful, and the abundance of the most affluent. Would you be concerned about the outcome of any of your endeavors? Of course not. So, imagine that you have all of that. What would you do? What would be possible? What would you change? How would you act on your inspiration?

The incredible reality is that you already have this power. It's already within you, and you are already using this power daily. If your present reality or circumstances are not what you desire, then you are not using this power effectively, and you are most likely not using this power consciously. So how do you use this power to get everything you desire?

The secret is as simple as learning how to think correctly. Really! You have two feelings, for the most part – pleasure and pain. They are both motivators. You want more joy and less pain. Everyone prefers to feel good versus bad, wouldn't you agree?

Have you ever had a day when everything went your way? It felt great. Did you feel great because everything went your way? Or did everything go your way because you felt great? The latter is likely the more accurate explanation of your fantastic day and every other day that you've considered phenomenal.

Your body and mind are united. They cannot live separate lives just as your physical and mental worlds are united. It is impossible for your physical world not to follow your mental world. Or another way to look at it is that your outer world follows your inner world.

There is no way for everything to go your way if you are in a horrible mood. Similarly, having a dreadful day is impossible when you have an optimistic attitude. Harmony in how you feel or your non-physical world will create harmony in your physical world.

In everything you accomplish, achieve, or becomes your reality, the following is true:

- You achieve only if you believe you can
- Your beliefs are consistent with who you are
- Who you are is shaped by what you think

What you think leads to whom you become, and what you become leads to what you achieve or attract into your life. But there's more to it than that because we must consider the entire Universe in this equation. This becomes more complicated to explain, but the result is still as simple as thoughts create your beliefs and create what you become, and your beliefs and who you have become create your expectations. In due course, your expectations create actions and circumstances consistent with your thoughts every time.

Wouldn't it be nice if, when you had a thought, everyone and everything in the Universe responded to your thoughts as if they were commands that must be followed?

Of course, that would be amazing! Not only would that be amazing, but that is the potential with which you have been empowered. Not in some future time and place, but right here, right now!

Do you believe in a Higher Power? Do you believe that our Higher Power, the Divine, is in each of us? There is no doubt in my mind. Science supports the miracle of life. This Universal Energy that unites us all has power. We are connected with the Divine through our subconscious mind, and we all have this connection.

The Divine, the Infinite, the Universal Mind or Energy, the Holy Spirit, the All-Powerful, the Universal Substance, and our Eternal Energy are words used to name God's magical, mysterious power. The Universal Mind is the life principle of every atom that exists. Every atom is intelligent and seeks to carry out the purpose for which it was created. It is All-Powerful, creative by nature, always present, and the powerful force behind our connectedness or oneness with all in the Universe. So, when you think consciously or subconsciously, you connect with everyone and everything in the Universe through your connection to the Universal Mind or the God within us. It is Omnipotent Law.

Most people live only in their physical or outer world, yet it is the non-physical spirit of the Universe within you that creates everything in the physical world.

The Universal Mind is not objective but subjective. It does not judge your beliefs and determine whether it will cooperate with you; this Universal Energy connects your beliefs to everyone and everything in the Universe so that you can deliver the result of your beliefs in your physical world.

Therefore, if you believe it, you will attain it, whether or not it is what you want. Everyone and everything in the Universe instinctively, without conscious thought, responds to your thoughts and beliefs and will provide you with an environment or situation consistent with your beliefs.

Each individual is a part of this Universal Energy. Universal Energy creates only through the individual, and the individual can create only through Universal Energy.

Correlating this for those who believe in God or Jesus Christ, the Holy Spirit within you connects with the Spirit within each of us. Some people say that God uses all of us to answer the prayers of others. He creates everything through the individuals.

The circumstances of situations that occur do so because of your thoughts. Let's look at an example, such as your body weight. Your weight today is a result of the behavior and actions of your recent past. Your recent behavior reflects your current beliefs resulting from your past thoughts. Ultimately, your past thoughts created the chain of events that resulted in your current weight.

However, if you decide today that you will lose weight and know that failure is not an option, you immediately begin to change your thoughts. The changes include how you think about your food intake and exercise, among other things. Your beliefs know that improvements in this regard will result in weight loss.

In this example, only after your behavior changes will the result begin to manifest physically. So if you start acting as if you're one hundred thirty pounds when you are two hundred pounds, you will eventually become one hundred thirty pounds. But if you continue to believe that you can't lose weight, this will affect your behavior, and change won't occur.

In The Official Guide to Success, Tom Hopkins says, "Fake it until you make it." [5] If you act like you're already where you want to be, the physical reality will follow.

In this analogy, your behavior in the physical world brings about the desired result. But what if you need others for the desired effect to be attained? What if you didn't know what to do to achieve the desired result? The good news is that the same approach still works. Your connection with Universal Energy will help you find your way.

Your thoughts will shape your beliefs, and your beliefs will attract the circumstances and situations in your physical world needed to bring about your desired result. However, what is most important to understand is that the energy of beliefs is All-Powerful and permeates everything and everyone in the Universe, not only your physical actions but also those of others.

By understanding this, you begin to partner with Universal Energy in designing your own life's reality. You co-create with the All-Mighty!

Every result or effect in your outer world has been caused by your thoughts and orchestrated through Universal Energy. When you believe something, you are in direct alignment with attracting it. Your beliefs connect with the Universe through Universal Energy, which permeates everything and everyone. This mental action and reaction are the *Law of Causation.*

So, imagine that it will become if you think it, believe it, and expect it. There is a difference between hoping for something and knowing it will result. Using the weight loss example again, when you decide that you will accomplish your weight-loss goal, and you know that nothing will prevent you from achieving it, when you genuinely know and expect it as sure as the sun rising in the morning, then you attain it, don't you?

If you say, 'I'll try to lose weight' or 'I'll give it a shot,' that is permitting yourself to fail, and that is not the same as knowing you'll lose weight and likely will not achieve your goal. Your thoughts lack belief. You must have faith that your desired result is inevitable, or you will achieve what you know is certain.

Your physical world is observed through your senses and then interpreted by your conscious mind. Through your thoughts, your conscious mind makes conclusions about happenings, and the conclusions shape your beliefs. Once a belief is fully formed, it is stored in the subconscious mind. The subconscious doesn't make decisions about whether something is true or false or if something is right or wrong. The subconscious takes the conclusions of the conscious mind as fact.

When you observe through your senses and interpret things constructively, you build a constructive belief that your entire body feels. It feels good and results in a harmonious state in your physical and non-physical worlds. That belief is then deposited into the subconscious mind for future use.

If you interpret things as destructive, you build a harmful belief, which is also felt by your entire body. This doesn't feel good. It doesn't feel good because your emotions tell you that your interpretation was incorrect. The siren goes off because you exit the emergency exit door in error. Esther and Jerry Hicks, the authors of Ask and It is Given, call it your 'Emotional Guidance System.'[6] If you don't feel good, your Emotional Guidance System is telling you that you have misinterpreted things and are shaping the wrong beliefs, which will bring about the bad result or future reality.

How can two people observe the same things but interpret them differently? This is usually a result of their current beliefs. When you consciously control your thoughts, you shape your beliefs. Once a belief is accepted as fact it will ultimately instinctively be used by the subconscious mind and Universal Energy. Your beliefs connect with Universal Energy, which connects your beliefs to the entire Universe.

Suppose your subconscious mind communicates through Universal Energy to everyone and everything in the Universe. In that case, everyone unconsciously begins to rearrange their lives to create a circumstance consistent with your belief. Pretty compelling and impressive.

Your connection to Universal Energy is always powerful and present, whether you realize it or not. When you think, you activate the power of Universal Energy accordingly. Every thought, therefore, is the cause of a reaction. You think something, and Universal Energy begins to act through vibrations instantly, and there will eventually be a reaction accordingly. Because of this, it is essential that you control your thoughts as you prompt Universal Energy to work on your behalf and ultimately deliver to you the conditions that are in alignment with your thoughts.

There will always be a reaction to your thoughts every time. It is the only way you create anything in your life. It is the only way anything is made in the Universe. All power is under your control through your thoughts and beliefs. When you thoroughly understand this Omnipotent Law, you can apply it to all conditions, which is the basis for all physical things.

The non-physical eternal being that you are creates everything in the physical world. We live through our conscious thoughts and subconscious reactions, which are connected to everyone and everything in the Universe through Universal Energy or the Spirit within each of us.

Somehow we have been conditioned, and most of us today subconsciously believe, that the outer world has the solutions to change. The outer world is what creates opportunities for us and the circumstance we are living with today.

However, that is untrue. For example, if you are ill, medical care treats the symptoms or the physical cause of the illness. Omnipotent Law says that you must change the thinking and belief of the individual, and the physical world will respond accordingly. Without a change in belief, the medical solution will not cure the cause. But if you believe the medical solution will cure the cause, then and only then will it.

Remember, you already have this power, and it is always working. Your reality today is a result of your thoughts and beliefs. You have co-created your current reality with the cooperation of Universal Energy. It is that simple.

If you're unhappy with your current reality, you have deposited beliefs into your subconscious mind that are not aligned with your true desires. Therefore, you have used this power unintentionally to prevent you from attaining your true desires.

Listen to your 'Emotional Guidance System.' When you don't feel good about something, your thoughts are not aligned with what you want. That bad feeling is your siren warning you that your thoughts are communicating with Universal Energy and what ultimately will be delivered to you if you don't change course are circumstances that are not going to feel good.

The only way to maximize the power within to attract what you truly desire is in a harmonious state. Think about it... your weight-loss program won't work if you keep focusing on how it won't work or that you don't want to do what you've set out to do. When you focus on it not working, you don't feel great about starting your weight-loss program, do you? There's a conflict between your goal and your thoughts and beliefs; therefore, you're not in a harmonious state. Thus, there's no way that you'll be successful.

When you're mentally efficient, your thoughts feel good and align with your desired result. Your non-physical being is in a harmonious state. All is good. The more you can stay unified, the more you align with the Universe's forces that will bring you circumstances that are consistent with your desires.

How do you intentionally feel harmonious?

It's all about controlling your thoughts and interpreting everything with a positive spin so that you develop constructive beliefs that will work to your advantage versus your detriment. Have faith and know that the way you have decided to view the situation will be your truth and your reality.

The great news is that by applying Omnipotent Law, you can substitute any favorable situation for a negative one, abundance for poverty, wisdom for ignorance, pleasure for pain, and freedom for oppression. You can attract anything you desire and have the discipline to pursue.

Meditation Exercise One

This exercise aims to master securing control of your physical body. You must be able to control your body before you progress to the next chapter.

Take your position as described in the Introduction and relax. Inhale deeply, and exhale slowly. Feel your stomach rise with each inhale and fall as you exhale. Keep every other body part perfectly still. Let your thoughts roam where they will yet recognize your breathing and what it does to your body when you breathe deeply.

Do this for no less than ten minutes. Continue this once or twice daily for a minimum of four days or until you secure complete control of your physical body. You must master stillness and have a strong understanding of this chapter before progressing to the next chapter and exercise.

The Power of the Subconscious Mind

Chapter Two

Most know that our mind operates in two modes, consciously and subconsciously. The conscious mind deals with things in your outer world. It reasons and therefore has limited capacity and processes relatively slowly.

The subconscious mind deals with your inner world. It perceives by intuition and absolutes and processes rapidly. It has unlimited capacity due to its unity with the Divine. Our subconscious mind makes decisions so effectively and efficiently that it always makes the correct decision based upon the absolute guidelines it has been given to follow.

The conscious mind cannot function in the same manner as the subconscious. When you stop and think about something, this slows down the processing time. Imagine what would happen if we had to consciously make every decision associated with the operations of our vital organs. At our present conscious capacity, we could never be able to sustain our own lives.

We don't have time to think about whether it's time to take a breath or whether our heart should pump some blood right now.

Relying upon your conscious mind for all mental functions would be similar to depending upon a nut for your annual nourishment, yet most people attempt to do that today.

Your conscious mind doesn't have the capacity or power that the subconscious does. When comparing the conscious mind to the power of the subconscious, the subconscious is still very unexplainable and accomplishes incredible tasks and results. How the subconscious works is still a mystery.

The value that the subconscious mind provides is enormous. It is a warehouse of memories and facts, principles and dreams. It inspires us and instinctively directs us. It's artistic and creative and stores our ideals.

Physical, spiritual, and mental power all comes from our subconscious. The physical power the subconscious mind provides is its ability to operate vital processes, with the preservation of your physical life and all life, including restoration of health. Yes, that's correct! The physical power of the subconscious mind includes the ability to heal. This physical power is something within you that starts at conception. The competent cells within your body know how to heal, which is their natural state.

The spiritual power of the subconscious is the source of your dreams, aspirations, and imagination. It is united with the Divine, and the more we recognize our connection to the Divine, the more powerful our relationship becomes and the more we can use it for the benefit of ourselves and others.

The subconscious mind's mental power is the ability to memorize and store knowledge. It is what controls your initiative and stores your beliefs. It is the warehouse for your habits.

Your subconscious mind is always working, and it works with precision regularly. Everything that you do with ease and perfection is done through your subconscious. It is believed that it is through the subconscious that the most creative genius resides.

The physical power of your subconscious is the dimension that your conscious mind can significantly influence. Your subconscious mind acts as if all decisions and beliefs developed by the conscious mind are valid. It doesn't judge or question, as it doesn't have time for that. Like a perfect computer program, your subconscious mind processes based on how the program was written, and your conscious mind writes and re-writes the program. Therefore, what you believe to be accurate, your subconscious acts upon it as if it is true every time.

Think of all the things we do without thought – walking, blinking, digesting, breathing, etc. We use our five senses without thinking about how we process what we see, feel, hear, touch and smell. We would have difficulty consciously stopping some of the things our subconscious routinely operates. Have you tried to stop your heart from beating or your blood from circulating? Not that I'd want you to do that, your subconscious won't allow it.

What about our youth? Can they stop themselves from growing or forming nerve or muscle tissue? Of course not. The physical power of the subconscious has an instinctive nature to preserve life, grow and heal.

Imagine if your subconscious had to think whether there was a right or wrong way for you to breathe or a right or wrong way for your heart to pump your blood. Your subconscious processes methodically and precisely without considering the possibility of whether it's doing it right or wrong.

The subconscious doesn't argue or even understand the difference between right and wrong or truth and fiction. It accepts everything as fact. Therefore, when you do something over and over, it becomes mechanical and is no longer an act of judgment by the conscious mind. It becomes a belief planted in your subconscious and is called upon instinctively without thought by your subconscious when needed.

This, of course, is awesome if the belief planted is empowering and consistent with your desires. However, it is harmful when the seed of thought is disempowering or based upon fear or any other painful emotion. It is essential to recognize the omnipotence of the subconscious mind and realize that this belief will be carried out regardless of whether it is pleasurable, painful, or even something you want.

How does the subconscious differ from the conscious mind? The conscious mind only deals with interpretations of the physical world through your five senses. It determines your beliefs associated with what you observe and has the power of reasoning. When you consider 'free will,' your conscious mind makes the choices for you.

Your conscious mind can direct your subconscious. The conscious mind interprets everything in the outer so that your subconscious can work like an efficient flawless machine relying upon the thoughts and beliefs planted by the conscious mind as fact. Our conscious mind protects our subconscious from all that is seen and observed while interpreting the information instead of taking it at face value.

For example, if you overhear a conversation that you completely disagree with, the fact that you consciously disagree is the truth planted in the subconscious mind. Your subconscious relies upon it as fact. Your conscious interpretation of the conversation gets buried in the subconscious mind. In this way, your conscious mind protects your subconscious from suggestions you disagree with and directs your subconscious actions to be consistent with your interpretations.

Remember that the subconscious mind never sleeps; it must be awake to keep the vital physical functions operating. Therefore, the conscious mind must protect the subconscious from outside influences. I once read about the concerns associated with your subconscious mind during surgery. General anesthesia knocks you out from a conscious perspective, but not from a subconscious perspective, as your vital organs continue to operate. Therefore, when you're influenced by general anesthesia, your subconscious is open to absorbing all that occurs without the filter of the conscious mind. Your conscious mind does not participate in shaping the suggestions made to the subconscious mind. Ultimately, when the conscious mind is not interpreting and shaping the recommendations to the subconscious mind, then the subconscious is left open to all the directions it experiences.

In summary, your conscious mind interprets through the five senses, then reasons, creating and shaping your beliefs. The subconscious mind operates instinctively upon those beliefs. The instincts in which the subconscious mind operates are shaped by the past reasoning of your subconscious mind.

Therefore, when your conscious mind interprets things and those interpretations are empowering, healthy, and constructive, your subconscious mind reaches accurate conclusions and is in harmony with Universal Energy, which is All-Powerful.

However, if your interpretations are disempowering, unhealthy, and destructive, your subconscious mind creates fear, worry, guilt, and many other destructive feelings and is not in harmony with Universal Energy. This is the cause of most mental and physical illnesses.

How do you eliminate disempowering, unhealthy, destructive beliefs? You suggest new empowering thoughts and feelings that will counteract the current beliefs. It can be as simple as stating specific, new, empowering suggestions or things you want to accomplish. The subconscious is naturally creative and connected to Universal Energy. The subconscious unites us with Omnipotence and will at once begin to work on your behalf with your new empowering thoughts and set the forces in an operation that will lead to the desired result. The more passion and feeling you can include in your new empowering suggestions, the more believable they will be and the more impact they will have. Your subconscious will accept the new thought as a new belief.

While you're having this conversation with yourself, in the back of your mind, you are thinking that the words you're saying are not valid, then understand, that is the belief you will develop.

Omnipotent Law is powerful. Those who have learned to master this law find harmony in situations and circumstances that others would expect to be complicated. Those who have learned to trust the power of the subconscious mind find that they have Infinite resources at their command – a direct connection to the Divine.

There is a difference between simply interpreting what comes our way and proactively directing our thoughts consciously, methodically, and constructively. When we proactively control our thoughts appropriately, we're in harmony with Universal Energy and begin to consciously be part of the creating process. The word 'constructively' is significant here. Universal Energy is harmonious. Destructive thoughts can never be in harmony with Universal Energy. This is what causes pain and illness, mental and physical. But when we direct our deliberate, empowering, constructive thoughts, we align with the harmony of Universal Energy and therefore align with the Divine. Natural law takes over.

Universal Energy is creative. It is the Creator. If the subconscious is united with Universal Energy, then it must be the same in form, nature, and quality as Universal Energy to some degree. Therefore, our subconscious mind is creative and will automatically correlate with its object of desire and bring it into manifestation. This law is called the *Law of Attraction*, which is how the subconscious mind will change circumstances or conditions on your behalf.

"We are not creatures of circumstances; we are creators of circumstance."

~Benjamin Disraeli

Meditation Exercise Two

In meditation exercise one, you mastered securing control of the physical body. Now you're going to begin to control your thoughts.

Go to your room and get into position as reviewed in the Introduction. Be perfectly still as you were in Exercise One, then begin to hinder most thoughts. When you have a thought pop into your head, clear it immediately. This isn't easy if you are not used to controlling your thoughts.

One of the ways you can inhibit unwanted thoughts is to focus on your breathing. As you inhale, think about oxygen permeating every part of your body. As you exhale, count your exhales and envision all impurities leaving your body. As a new thought enters your mind, erase it and refocus on your breathing and oxygen permeating every part of your body and impurities exiting your body each time you exhale.

Counting your breath can also help hinder unwanted thoughts. Count to three as you inhale, and count to four as you exhale. Think about the air entering your lungs and negativity and impurities leaving your body as you exhale.

Being able to hinder thoughts will ultimately give you control over all thoughts and will enable you to direct your thoughts to only those you desire. Complete this exercise a minimum of six times until you can inhibit your thoughts and keep your thoughts directed to your breathing.

Before progressing to Chapter Three, you must master this exercise and understand this chapter strongly.

Our Bodies Are Miracles

Chapter Three

Like the relationship between the conscious and subconscious minds is the relationship between the corresponding nervous systems. The cerebrospinal system is the organ of the conscious mind, and the sympathetic nervous system is that of the subconscious mind.

The cerebrospinal system has its center in the brain and is the channel through which we consciously perceive or interpret through our five senses and control the movement of our bodies.

The sympathetic nervous system has its autonomous cluster of nerve cells at the back of the stomach and below the diaphragm, known as the celiac plexus or solar plexus. The solar plexus is the channel through which we subconsciously control most vital functions of our bodies, such as the lower part of the esophagus, pancreas, kidneys, liver, gallbladder, intestines, and stomach, for example.[7]

Mystics believe that the solar plexus chakra influences ego, intuition, personality, and your zest for life, among others, and directly reacts to your thoughts, which is how destructive, disempowering thoughts can directly affect your health. When your solar plexus is distressed, it can cause many health issues, such as heartburn, stomach pain, nausea, and acid reflux, to name a few milder symptoms. More severe impacts could result in the development of eating disorders, hypoglycemia, and even diabetes.[8]

Emotionally, it can result in feelings of helplessness, an excessive need for control, a victim mentality, and self-esteem and self-identity issues. [8]

Although science has recognized that negative emotions affect physical health,[9] it's about impossible to prove this to be true or untrue. However, anecdotal evidence supports this belief as it is evident that those that work solar plexus chakra healing practices are more mindful, intuitive, and physically healthy. Those that are angry, stressed, and full of anxiety have a weakened immune system which leads to more disease.[10]

Every thought is received by the brain and then subjected to your interpretation by the conscious mind. The conclusion of your interpretation becomes a belief or a truth for you, and that belief is planted in your subconscious mind. We have already learned that the subconscious doesn't reason or question things; it simply acts upon your truths and beliefs.

The solar plexus is considered the 'sun' of the body because it is the central point for energy to be distributed to the body. If the energy emitted from our sun is intense, then the individual is considered magnetic and charismatic. These individuals regularly influence others positively. You can feel their light and positive energy.

When the solar plexus emits intense energy, it radiates this vibrantly through the three dimensions of the subconscious: the physical, spiritual, and mental. The solar plexus provides the physical energy and vitality needed to sustain life. It radiates energy through the vagus nerve to the brain, which also provides us with spiritual energy. Everything in life is energy, and the solar plexus nerve energy, with its ability to operate independently of the brain, is truly remarkable.

Additionally, the solar plexus provides the mental energy the conscious mind needs. The conscious mind depends on the subconscious to support thought. Suppose the solar plexus is not emitting intense energy. In that case, the body isn't receiving what it needs to heal itself, the connection with the brain and Universal Energy is interrupted, and thoughts affect our mental health.

The solar plexus is where we, as finite beings, are united with the Infinite and where we, as eternal beings, are connected with Eternal Energy.

In summary, our conscious mind develops and stores our beliefs in the subconscious mind. In the second brain, our gut brain, the energy radiated from the solar plexus is vital to this process as it is the center of energy in which we are united with Universal Energy. The solar plexus radiates energy to everything in the body and beyond. The quality, character, and nature of our thoughts determine the quality, character, and nature of our energy being radiated. Therefore, our conscious mind develops what is emitted to the Universe. It is our conscious mind that influences Omnipotent Power.

Think about it for a moment... when you are one with Infinite Power, you can overcome any situation or circumstance by the power of your thoughts. When you consciously realize this power, you will have nothing to fear, and you can co-create your life with the Divine.

Exploring this in more depth is it's empowering, positive, non-resistant thought, that expands your solar plexus and produces intense energy to your body and subconscious mind. Disempowering, negative, resistant thoughts contract your solar plexus and drains the energy. All you must do is let your sunlight shine.

There are two categories of thoughts: one feels pleasurable, and the other feels painful. When your thoughts are pleasant, your inner sun shines and emits abundant energy. When your thoughts are negative and feel painful, clouds hide your sun, and your energy is drained with little left over for your body's health or mental clarity. What types of thoughts create a feeling of pain? Some fear generates every painful thought. This cannot be oversimplified, as it is fear that you must eliminate from your thoughts. Fear is your devil. Worry, guilt, criticism, etc., are all fearful feelings.

I received a message from an associate in which she attempted to explain why she didn't like her life right now. Below is a small portion of that message:

"…I may hate every second of it, but I always get through it… I just hate where I am right now, but it's the life I'm stuck in, so… you breathe through it and pretend and hope and pray the next life will be better… no-bid deal, it's always been this way."

This type of belief and self-talk will ensure that the future delivers the life you're 'stuck in,' and not only has it 'always been this way,' but it always will if this is the belief that has been planted into the subconscious mind as truth.

What you believe will determine your experience. If you are dissatisfied with your present situation in life, the only way to change it is to change your belief. If you expect nothing, you'll get nothing. If you expect greatness, you'll get greatness. The Omnipotent Power of the Divine is within you and will ultimately deliver precisely what you have faith in expecting.

Let's consider the question, "Whom do you say that I AM?" This isn't simply a question from Jesus to Peter. This is the question that everyone must answer themselves. In other words, 'Who do you say that you are?' Your conviction and belief in yourself will determine your expression in life. However, your answer to this question is precisely what determines your experience in life.

Your thoughts, which create your beliefs, are seen to be recognizing yourself to be what you expect for yourself. To consciously think of being poor and to hope for wealth will do nothing but deliver to you what you are conscious of being, which is lacking. 'Shutting the door' is shutting out what you are now aware of being and claiming yourself to be what you desire.

Instead of hoping for the desired result, you must expect it. Have faith and know it will be delivered. Know that wealth is your destiny and that your current circumstances are only a result of your past thoughts. Today, everything has changed. Today, it is only a matter of time before Omnipotent Power will deliver evidence of your wealth. The very moment that your desire becomes an expectation, the moment that it becomes what you know to be true for you and is a point of conviction, at that very moment, you begin to draw the evidence of your claim into your life.

> "Faith is putting all your eggs in God's basket, then counting your blessings before they hatch."

> ~Ramona C. Carroll

Whatever the subconscious believes to be true is delivered to everyone and everything in the Universe as accurate, and the Infinite Power of the Universe provides evidence of that truth.

To apply this astonishing truth to your life, you must practice like anything else you have learned. It would be best if you first created empowering beliefs with your desires being the expected result. The most simple and effective way is to consciously concentrate on the object of your desire, not the lack thereof.

Identifying how you will produce the evidence of your newfound truth isn't necessary. As a finite being, with limitations of the conscious mind, you can't possibly determine the most creative solution. You must have faith in the Omnipotent Power of Universal Energy, which has unlimited resources and be open to the opportunities that will be presented.

Meditation Exercise Three

Now that you've mastered controlling your physical body and inhibiting thought, we will take it further. This time, you are to remain still, inhibit thought, and then add to your state by relaxing all the muscles and nerves in your body, releasing all tension.

Physical relaxation is a voluntary exercise of the conscious mind and enables the blood to circulate freely throughout the body and to and from the brain. Tension leads to abnormal mental activity, which some call restless mind syndrome.

If you find relaxing your body difficult, try to concentrate on feeling the pulse in your big toes one foot at a time. Once you feel it, stay focused on the pulse while you relax your feet. If a new thought pops into your mind, move to thoughts about your heels and again try to find and feel the pulse in your heels. Stay focused on the pulse and relax your body.

Again, move your thoughts to your knees if a new thought enters your mind. Concentrate on finding and feeling the pulse in your knees and relax your knees and legs. Continue this process on multiple body parts whenever a new thought enters your mind. You will find fewer interruptions of thought and an ability to release all tension in every part of your body.

Continue this until your body is completely relaxed, restful, and at peace with you and the world.

Relaxing every part of your body, and controlling your thoughts, is like rebooting a computer. The subconscious mind begins to operate from a fresh new perspective, and the solar plexus can resume working efficiently and instinctively.

The Spirit of the 'I' Within

Chapter Four

Many people contemplate who they are. You hear comments such as, 'I want to find myself.' Who is 'I' in this question? Is the 'I' your mind? Certainly not. The mind is like a computer that reasons and plans, but the mind doesn't have logic or the ability to think.

Is the 'I' your body? Although the 'I' tells your body what to do, it is something beyond.

What about your personality? The 'I' isn't your personality, either. Your core personality is developed over time based on all your life experiences, knowledge, and everything and everyone you have experienced since inception. However, the 'I' within you determines your likes and dislikes, which results in your personality.

When you say, 'I want' or 'I think,' the 'I' tells the mind what it wants or thinks. The 'I' instructs the body what to do and the 'I' determines your preferences, which create your personality.

> *"We are not human beings on a spiritual journey.*
> *We are spiritual beings on a human journey."*
>
> ~Stephen Covey

The 'I' is spiritual and the source of all power. When you say, 'I want to find myself.' You are saying that your Spirit, this 'I' within you and your inner voice, is not in alignment with the physical or outer world.

The most extraordinary power that your Spirit has is the power to think, and it is this power that shapes who you are and who you become.

Unfortunately, most of us haven't been taught how to think correctly, and therefore, we don't, which results in not attaining what we desire.

How do you think correctly? Every thought must consider all others in the Universe. Harm to anyone, including yourself, is not correct thinking. Every action or thought must benefit everyone involved and cannot be to anyone's detriment.

Many people think about acquiring things for selfish reasons. This is the germ that manifests negative results in your life. The more you think about serving others and realize that selfish thoughts are the poison that will kill any growth, the more you will come to know the true power of your thoughts.

You are part of the Universe. The 'I' within you is part of the Infinite. We are all connected, and as a part of the Infinite, we cannot provoke or alienate any other part of the Universe and benefit.

The happiness, peace, and harmony within the Universe depend upon each of us recognizing the interests of the Universe. So, everything affects everyone and everything in the Universe. Every action is felt throughout the Universe to some degree, yet you will never personally benefit from imposing harm on any part of the Universe.

This is one of the principles you must focus on to gain any form of happiness. The *Law of Reciprocity* – the Universe will deliver to you in an expanded proportion to what you provide to the Universe. With every thought if you keep this in mind, you will change your thoughts to be constructive and not waste time or money on things that don't work within this principle.

This becomes a habit through practice. Repetition is the mother of skill. If you aren't already a master of correct, constructive thinking, now is the time to teach yourself. *The Law of Fair Exchange* says that your result will be directly proportional to your effort. Therefore, you will benefit from learning and integrating this principle directly to the effort you extend in learning it right now.

Here's where you can start.

- I can be what I decide to be.
- I can be what I will myself to be.
- I can be what I desire to be.

Begin repeating these vision statements every morning, every night, and multiple times throughout the day until they become beliefs while keeping in mind who and what the 'I' really is. The spiritual 'I' understands you cannot gain by harming any other within the Universe.

Eventually, through repetition, this practice creates a new habit. Habits are formed by repeatedly doing or saying something until your subconscious has accepted it as a belief you instinctively act upon.

You will begin to believe these statements, and you will instinctively act upon this belief. When you instinctively act upon these statements of belief, and they are impregnated with love for everyone, you will become invincible.

Right now, try to pick up an object near you. Were you able to pick it up? Of course, you were. Trying is doing. Anything you try to do, you do. If you don't do it, it's because you didn't try; you decided not to do it. You either picked up the object or didn't; whichever you did was your choice. That choice begins to create habits that empower you or disempower you.

Don't try to do anything. To quote Nike, 'Just Do It' or don't do it, but don't say you'll try when you know you have no intentions of following through. This creates a habit of failure, one of the most disempowering habits you can make.

Below is the cycle of creating a new habit...

- Unconscious incompetence: We don't know what we don't know
- Conscious incompetence: We realize what we don't know.
- Conscious competence: If we consciously think about it, we can do it right.
- Unconscious competency: We don't have to give it much thought, and we can still do it correctly.

The unconscious competency stage is when a new thought has become a habit and becomes automatic. The subconscious mind considers it valid, and there is no longer any doubt about it.

For example, since this information is likely new to you, you may be at the conscious incompetence stage when it comes to thinking correctly. Practice, and perfect repetition, will progress your thinking to a conscious competency, and in due time, you will have created the habit of thinking correctly.

Let's relate this to habits of failure. Have you created a habit of failure? Instead of living your life based on the habit of failure, you can live your life based on the habit of success, which is a requirement for abundant living. What's the success habit? It is simple... do what you say you will do. Starting something with no intention of finishing creates a pattern of failure. Think about it. If you set achievable goals and don't follow through three out of four times, you have created a belief that you fail seventy-five percent of the time at whatever you decide to accomplish. This is highly disempowering.

Jim Rohn, a business philosopher I respect immensely, says, "*Something easy to do is also easy not to do.*" Don't get into the habit of not completing your easy predetermined goals. You create the habit of failure instead of the habit of success.

When you decide, you must follow through because the lack of following through creates the habit of failure. If this has been your past, change it today. Decide that you will repeat these vision statements morning, night, and several times throughout the day. You may want to commit to doing this for only two weeks. Then after you've been successful, extend it two more weeks, and so on.

Once you have committed yourself, you will have planted a seed of an empowering belief about your ability to be what you desire at will. You will also have planted a seed that can grow into a habit so deep within your subconscious that when your goal is more significant, your subconscious will kick in and execute based on your new habit of success.

Ultimately, do not say you'll 'try' to do something that you are capable of doing unless you are committed to following it through.

When you learn to do what you say you're going to do, not only will you gain credibility with everyone you encounter, but you will find the power within that controls your outer world; your reality, the power within that ultimately delivers to you in the outer world the evidence of your beliefs.

If you think about it, this isn't that surprising to consider. You are part of the Infinite, in which we are all united. Scientifically, nothing is more certain than that we are in the presence of an Infinite and Eternal Energy to which we are all connected.

Most religions consider God as being within us, as well. The Bible says, "Know ye not that ye are the temple of God, and that the Spirit of God dwelleth in you?" There are many times in the Bible that this is stated over and over again. 'I AM the Shepherd,' 'I and my Father are One.' And so on...

Here is the SECRET OF MASTERY: The Infinite is within you, is All-Powerful, has unlimited resources, and has everything in abundance. With this power, you can accomplish anything you desire that respects all parts of the Universe.

The first requirement of being of service to others is having the means to do so. You cannot be generous to others unless you have abundance. You cannot give and serve others unless you are strong. The Spirit within you has the right to the abundance in the Universe to be strong to help others. The Spirit within has access to all the abundance, and as long as you live within the *Law of Reciprocity* and the *Law of Love*, what you desire is within your command.

The Infinite expresses and creates through the individual, and the individual expresses through the Universe. When you're in alignment with all that is good and being of service to the Universe, the Spirit within you sets the forces in motion so that the Infinite can create through you. Seek inspiration and connect with your Spirit within.

Your Spirit within can deliver you your heart's desire. It is creative, and it is what brings you to life. Without Spirit, you are nothing. If your Spirit were to die or leave your body, you would cease to exist. Your Spirit will assist you in attracting abundance and will work to deliver to you the evidence of your beliefs. Your realization and acknowledgment that God is within you will allow you access to life's abundance.

If you recall, the cause behind all effects is within. Your Spirit is the part of you that is part of the Infinite. It is the part that is the Creator within your conscious influence. You must realize your conscious power due to your unity with this All-Powerful Spirit.

Your conscious thoughts create your habits and beliefs. They make your awareness of who you are or your awareness of being. So, it is crucial for you to understand your conscious power.

Seek silence and stillness often because if you quiet your mind and body, you can think correctly. It is thought that is the secret to creativity and, ultimately, your ability to manifest your desires.

The *Law of Vibration* carries light and electricity. We know it works even though we don't see it. Thought, similarly, is carried through the *Law of Vibration*. So thought vibrates beyond our physical being and is united with the Infinite.

Now consider the *Law of Love*. Love is directly aligned with the Infinite, so thoughts based on Love are given vitality.

The last law in this process is the *Law of Growth*. It's the law in which thoughts take form and expression. Emotions give feeling to thoughts so that thoughts will take shape. If you have a thought based upon the *Law of Love*, that thought is in direct alignment and united with the Infinite and takes form through the *Law of Growth*.

How do you develop the faith, courage, and passion for accomplishing this chain of events that will ultimately express your thoughts and desires to you? It's simple: practice and repetition.

Meditation Exercise Four

In this exercise, you'll mentally relax and let go of all stress and all negative feelings and thoughts. As always, do not progress to this exercise if you haven't mastered the ability to physically relax in Exercise Three.

Think of your computer, which has multiple processes running and gets locked up because there's so much going on that its memory can't handle it. So, you reboot your computer, and it begins to work again the way it was meant to work. That is what we're doing here. Your solar plexus needs to be radiating energy to every part of the body. Your conscious mind relies upon a radiating solar plexus for instinctive thought. When you reboot your system, your body and mind begin to process correctly again.

Take your normal position, still and relax your body. Take as much time necessary to relax the body and remain still. Simultaneously, inhibit outside thoughts, and then remove all tension in your mind.

Let go of all adverse conditions, such as hatred, anger, worry, jealousy, envy, sorrow, trouble, or disappointment. This may be difficult, but you cannot let your emotions control you right now; you must allow your intellect to take over and control your emotions. Release all negativities. You can let go of these things. Once you do, you will experience mental freedom.

The quality of your thought correlates to its object in your outer world. Your ability to consciously release all disempowering thoughts will lead to mental freedom and is the first step in allowing you to consciously direct your use of the universal *Law of Attraction* from which there is no escape.

As a reminder, you want to do this for no less than ten minutes daily. However, begin to lengthen the time to twenty minutes daily. Continue this exercise until you can quickly and easily get yourself in this state. Once you have mastered this, you will no longer be enslaved to your body and mind, and you are well on your way to your body and mind becoming enslaved to you.

The Conscious Choice of Your Heredity

Chapter Five

You have heard that most of us use only about ten percent of our mental power. That's because more than ninety percent of our mental power is subconscious, and most of us use only a tiny portion of our subconscious as we rely upon our conscious mind for most of our power. Yet the subconscious can solve anything and everything. So how do we tap into this power?

Let's first understand how you have come to be the person you have become. You recognize that your subconscious mind manages every part of your physical body and that your objective or conscious mind can influence your subconscious by creating new beliefs and expectations through your thoughts.

Heredity is the predominant source behind the mind that permeates the body. Heredity gives us our attitude, organ function, control over movement, blood circulation, nerve and muscle strength, bone structure, and many other physical things. Mentally, we are the total of everything and everyone we have experienced, including what has been passed onto us through all past generations. This is important to understand because it can play a massive role in the person you become.

Most of us accept our heredity without question, and that acceptance becomes who we are because we believe it is who we are. On the other hand, if you think that you will be different because what you expect of yourself and what you know you can become is unlike that of your past generations, then that is what you will become. You have a choice as to which of the inherited characteristics you embrace and which you do not. Those that are desirable, you should consciously use. For those that are undesirable, you need to get rid of them deliberately.

Today, you are the result of your past thinking, regardless of what you inherited, and you will become what you are thinking about today in the future. The *Law of Attraction* will bring what you think about, not what you desire, wish, or hope for, but what you focus on and have created in your mind's eye by your thoughts.

If the thoughts that consume your mind are of fear, doubt, negativity, apprehension, worry, guilt, etc., this will be the result of what enters your life. If the thoughts that enter your mind are happy, optimistic, positive, excited, abundant, enthusiastic, faithful, courageous, healthy, etc., that will be the result of what enters your life.

Ultimately, the quality of the thoughts you generate comes back to you and will be evident in the circumstances in your life, similar to a gravitational pull that attracts like.

The best physical scientists cannot account for initial creation or the origination of life, not through heredity or evolution. This Infinite Life flows through you, the power that comes from the 'I' within you that flows directly from the Infinite or Universal Energy in which we are all united.

You inherit your physical traits from your parents and all past generations. You inherit the power within you from the Infinite or Universal Energy in which you are in the image and likeness. Understand that this inheritance gives you power over weakness, fear, negativity, and intimidation.

This Infinite Power within you is active with use. You are the vessel in which the Infinite Power is differentiated into physical form. We've mentioned before that the Universe creates through the individual. Therefore, unless you give and allow the Infinite Power to create through you, the vessel is blocked, and you cannot receive its power. Use is a condition associated with inheriting this power. The more we give, the more we get. Remember the *Law of Reciprocity* and the *Law of Love*. The Universe will return to you in a multiplied proportion to what you give.

Complete a 'mental house-cleaning' every day. Mental, moral, and physical purity is essential to mastering empowering expectations and ultimately empowering realities. This is as simple as the choices you make. Suppose you choose to eliminate negative thoughts, refuse to have anything to do with them, and redirect your thoughts to those that are positive and empowering. In that case, that choice will deliver in your physical world situations and circumstances worthy of your thoughts.

You can have complete power over the circumstances that arise in your physical world by claiming in your thoughts the environment in which you insist upon living. You must not only have a desire but also claim it as yours and own it throughout your thoughts. Become it in consciousness. Health, harmony, and abundance are just a few rewards; the only requirement is the commitment to practice the skills that make the 'right' thinking a habit.

To attain more loving relationships, you must become more loving to others. You must be more abundant in what you do to attain more abundance. To achieve financial freedom, you must become free from financial burdens. All power is contingent upon adequately using the power already in your possession. Use this Infinite Power within you for the good of all, and you will become more powerful and not only give others more but simultaneously begin living an abundant life.

Meditation Exercise Five

For every meditation exercise, beginning with this exercise through the final meditation exercise, you are to start as follows:

- Still the body
- Still the mind
- Relax the body
- Relax (release) the mind

The next step is to visualize. The balance of the exercises will ask you to imagine a perfect picture. Before progressing to visualization, you must complete stilling and relaxing the body and mind.

Additionally, it is crucial to visualize the result desired, not how you get there or the lack thereof. If you envision your health, see yourself as vibrant and cured; if you want financial wealth, see yourself in your new home.

Some will consider meditation and visualization as prayer. If you are praying for another, see that person in the situation that you desire them to be in. For example, if you are praying for someone ill, in your mind's eye, envision the favorable desirable situation and give thanks for their healing.

In this meditation, you will transition from stilling and relaxing the mind and body to visualizing a pleasant situation. Make a complete mental picture of it. See the buildings, grounds, trees, friends, associations, and everything complete.

At first, you will probably think of everything under the sun except the ideal upon which you desire to concentrate. That's okay, but eventually, you want to picture your desired situation. Practice this meditation exercise every day without fail until you have it mastered. Continue to visualize the same desired result.

Our Thoughts Are Energy in Motion

Chapter Six

Universal Energy not only has unlimited resources but can produce unlimited results and has Infinite Intelligence.

"I am in perfect harmony with the working of the law. I stand aside and let Infinite Intelligence make easy and successful my way."

~Florence Scovel Shinn

Universal Energy can produce any result at any time for anyone. So how do we use this Infinite Power to make the desired results or circumstances?

Let's consider the effects of electricity as a parallel to understand the effects of Universal Energy better. The Universe today doesn't have any more electricity within its realm than it did in the 1800s. Yet today we have digital audio players, heat pumps, and power to our homes and businesses. The effects of electricity today are significantly improved over what most couldn't even imagine in the 1800s, and one hundred years from now, the effects of electricity will probably be much more significant.

Electricity is a form of energy in motion, and its effects depend upon the electrical device connected to this form of energy. This motion of energy through the attached device can create music, heat, cool air, light, and many other things depending upon the device. But without the audio player, electricity doesn't produce music; without electricity, the audio player doesn't make music. Without a compatible device and the proper wiring, electricity can't possibly produce a thing.

But as we learn and expand our understanding of the wiring and how we make things work with electricity, we create more opportunities for its use.

What is the effect of Universal Energy? Like electricity, Universal Energy, in which we are all connected, cannot produce anything independently. It requires thought. The Universe today doesn't have any more ability to create effects through thought than it did in the 1800s or will one hundred years from now. However, as we learn and expand our understanding and power of this Universal Energy, we create more opportunities through thought.

Thought is a form of energy in motion, like electricity or cellular service and its effect depends upon the device or mind with which the thought is connected. This energy in motion through the mind of an individual can create anything. The creations or effects produced are the result of the action and reaction of the individual upon the Universe through thought. The human brain makes all of this happen. The human brain is the thought device in which thoughts take form.

Every thought sets the brain cells in motion. However, concentrated thought sets the forces in motion to express your thought perfectly in form. Concentrated thought can cause the elimination of any undesirable circumstance and the attainment of any desirable occasion. Focused thought is the essential factor associated with the power within you. It is what will allow you to accomplish anything at will.

Concentrated thought is how you consciously visualize your desired result and hold it in your mind until it is planted into your subconscious and becomes part of who you are. Once you ascend in consciousness to whom you desire to be, and your desired result is part of who you are, you have the Spirit of Power that connects you with Universal Truth.

This sounds simple. Not necessarily. However, it can be learned. Try focusing on a single purpose for ten minutes. You may find that your mind roams, and you'll need to bring it back into focus. This roaming usually doesn't create the concentrated thought required to bring your thought into reality. Invest some time in the greatest invention ever, the human brain, and practice. Repetition is the mother of skill.

Fortunately, with practice, you will improve your ability in this regard significantly. Once you have mastered concentrating your thoughts on a single definite purpose in harmony with the Divine, the results will be excellent.

In the original *Master Key*, Charles Haanel compared the power of thought to that of a magnifying glass. If you focus it long enough with the sun's energy appropriately aligned, it is incredible what the magnifying glass can accomplish. Similarly, concentrated thought on a definite purpose aligned with our sun or in harmony with the Divine can produce results that are just amazing.

There is a tremendous mental world in which we live; it is united with Universal Energy, and it is All-Powerful. Our mental world will respond to our thoughts proportionate to our faith and purpose. The more the goal is in harmony with the Universe, meaning all that is good and constructive, without destruction to any part of the Universe, and the greater our faith and passion, the greater the strength to manifest.

Learn to remove yourself from the many activities and thoughts of your day-to-day life to have time for reflection and directive thinking. These are essential to generate a constructive mental attitude. You develop discernment and a more precise understanding and appreciation of facts. If you look within and focus on the universal laws that consistently deliver a predetermined result, you will eventually come into vibrational alignment with what is most desirable in life.

The most extraordinary ideas come to those who are receptive and open themselves up to receive. When you're in harmony with Universal Energy, you are united with everyone and everything in the Universe; with this harmony, you master the principles of thinking and connecting with Omnipotent Power.

In this harmonious state, your thoughts expand universally, and you will find that your environment and circumstances follow your mental and spiritual development. Begin by identifying the Spirit within you, and then the opportunity will be made available to you through perception, knowledge, and inspired thought. Knowledge sparks growth, and inspired thought will prompt action, which results in a transformation into Infinite and unlimited possibilities.

Meditation Exercise Six

This exercise begins to work on visualization techniques. Get a photograph or use an image of someone you love immensely in your life on your phone or tablet. Bring it to your room, get into position, and study the photograph carefully. Note each feature, eye color, shape, feeling, and even any birth marks, freckles or lines on their face. Now close your eyes and meditate as you learned in meditation exercises one through four.

Once you're in a meditative state with your muscles, nerves, and mind relaxed, try to see that someone you love in your mind's eye. See your loved one mentally in the same level of detail. Are you able to picture them perfectly? If you can, that's awesome! You are well on your way to using the power of visualization.

If you're not there yet, repeat this until you can create the picture in your mind's eye that significantly resembles the photograph.

This exercise will prepare your mind for a new habit that you will work on creating. Visualization is one of the primary techniques you will use to control or direct your thoughts and is the primary tool used when concentrating on a definite purpose that you desire to manifest.

Dream Perfect Dreams

Chapter Seven

Your imagination is potent and the primary process you'll use to design your future. Whatever picture you can vividly imagine in your mind's eye can become your reality. Can you dream? Can you imagine and create without limitation? If you can, you can attract it into your life.

Like planning a successful business, you must plan for a successful life. Therefore, the first step in the planning process is to decide. You must decide what you want. Effective visualization or the idealization of the perfect plan will be your guide in that process.

This could be the most challenging step for some, but it is essential. Meditation is needed to give you the clarity of thinking you'll need and is the method by which concentrated thought becomes powerful. There are no limitations except for those you have placed upon yourself. Your power to think is unlimited; therefore, through Universal Energy, your power to create your reality is also unlimited, so throw out all preconceived notions of what can and cannot be. There are no limitations in your imagination.

Your goal is to define the desired result clearly. Don't get attached to the means, just the result. Now hold that image in your mind and do it daily. You must commit to visualization daily. This commitment will generate the concentration and focus that will deliver your dreams to reality.

Concentrating thoughts on a definite purpose will unknowingly set the forces in motion to deliver the evidence of your being. A general picture may be where you start. Then the details will gradually unfold and take shape until progressively, you hold a clear view of your result, which will eventually materialize in your physical world.

If you have difficulties creating your perfect picture in your mind, make it using today's technology in a slide show or movie and then continue to watch the movie, this will spark the fire that will allow you to see the light, which will deliver a clear mental picture for your imagination to expand upon.

A movie isn't the answer. However, the images in your mind, including you in the picture, will influence your subconscious mind to accept it as truth. Think about the Universe and all its abundance for a moment. Could the Universe be created by accident? No, not likely.

Now consider the higher power behind this incredible creation that ultimately created the Universe and that we are united with the same Universal Mind as that of the creator. That same Universal Mind created the Universe operating through the individual or you and gives you the power to create your reality.

Anything created today is being created through the individual. Any new product, service, or invention is first imagined in the mind of its creator. And a great athlete or performer imagines their perfect performance before it comes to fruition. Any great architect conceives the structure they intend to build before it is put to paper and in its final form. And all of these cases, the picture of the desired result must first be vivid in thought before it ever can be reality.

Similarly, you must have a clear, vivid picture of the desired result as you wish it to be. Savor the feeling of enjoying your life this way. Imagine that you have already achieved it and are now living it. You must ascend in consciousness and become whom you desire to be.

Not only does imagining things from this perspective allow you to understand what will become of your future, but you will also develop faith, confidence, endurance, courage, and enthusiasm for your desires. You will develop a passion for your desires and life.

Begin to dream perfect dreams. Don't worry about the current reality. Imagine a beautiful, abundant world with peace and happiness, where everything goes your way, and begin to be the person in your perfect dream. The Universe will correspond to your command. Life will be rearranged and become what you have imagined for you.

"All breaks you need in life wait within your imagination. Imagination is the workshop of your mind, capable of turning mind energy into accomplishment and wealth."

~Napoleon Hill

Visualize the perfect image and hold it in your mind. Feel the way it feels. The rest will unfold, and you will be led to your desires. You will be given opportunities to expand and develop into what you desire. You will be inspired to take a path at the right time to achieve the desired effect.

Why have we been taught to look to our outer world for strength? We have been taught that it is the things we do that give us power and results. This is not the truth. It's not some supernatural power that only the fortunate few are blessed with; everyone has this ability.

You have millions of brain cells and billions of competent cells in your body. Each of these cells has the intelligence to act upon any suggestion, and they have the psychic ability to attract whatever is necessary to carry out any suggestion. They do this through the *Law of Attraction* and silently attract what they need to survive. They take your suggestions as truth and attract what they need to accomplish your vision.

You know people who want money, power, health, and abundance but never seem to realize it. The issue in most cases is that they are trying to attain what they desire by doing something in the outer world without focusing upon their inner world. They think that they can achieve what they want by changing something in the outer world instead of changing who they are in their inner world. They need to realize how to bring the *Law of Attraction* into action. They never seek answers from their Spirit that can dream perfect dreams and has unlimited resources. They don't understand that looking for wisdom, peace, and truth from within is the key to setting the *Law of Attraction* into operation.

Wisdom will open the source of power that will manifest in thought and purpose, creating your desired reality.

If you imagine debt and continually think about it, concentrating on it over and over, worried about it, not only will your situation not improve, but it will also lead to more outstanding debt. Through the *Law of Attraction*, concentrating on debt brings about more debt.

If you imagine wealth and continually think about it, concentrating on it over and over, making decisions with the wisdom of the wealthy, and being excited about it, you guessed it. Your situation will improve. It will lead to wealth. Through the *Law of Attraction*, concentrating on wealth brings about more wealth.

Think about this for a moment: have you ever met a person who believes, 'I can't ever get a break?' That person's right, aren't they? What about the clumsy person who says, 'I'm so clumsy.' That person is regularly clumsy, aren't they?

On the other hand, do you know anyone who believes everything always seems to go right for them? That person is usually right as well.

"If you think you can, or if you think you cannot,

you are always right."

~Henry Ford

So why is it so challenging to think about what you desire as if you already have it versus thinking about the desire as something that you are lacking? Many tend to be too anxious and have anxiety, fear, or worry about things.

You must make the investment and stay focused on what's desired through meditation and visualization, and then allow the investment to grow. You must practice. Create the picture, dream the dream, throw away any preconceived notions of limitations, and be who it is you desire to be in consciousness. This does not mean doing nothing. You must act upon inspired thought that leads you toward your desires. Opportunities will be delivered to you, and you will have become the person you desire to be in consciousness. Then as the opportunities arise, you will instinctively act upon them.

Ask yourself this, and then be patient and reflect upon your thoughts and beliefs. 'Do you now and then feel the Spirit within you?' Does the spiritual 'I' within you determine your direction, or do you follow the crowd? Please don't allow the negativity of others, and their preconceived limited beliefs, to become your thoughts and, therefore, your reality. You can do anything you will yourself to be!

Exercise Meditation Seven

In meditation exercise 6, you began visualization techniques. You were asked to get a photograph of someone in your life whom you love and to visualize this photo in every detail. Can you picture the image in your mind's eye? If you can, then feel free to progress. Otherwise, continue with exercise 6 until you have mastered it.

Now take your position, and with this same image, visualize your loved one. See this person as you saw them last. Recall the conversation you had and imagine the person's face. See it distinctively. Now talk to your loved one about a mutual interest. See the expression on their face and how it changes. Here your loved one talk and watch them smile. Can you do this?

If you can, spark their interest by telling them a story about an adventure or trip. Talk to your loved one about something you want to do with them as if you had already been there and you're now sharing your experience with them. See your loved one's face light up with this spirit of fun or excitement. Feel their excitement. Feel your passion.

Can you do all of this? If not, with practice, you will get there. Once you can do this, you will consciously improve your imagination, which is exceptional progress toward mastering the *Law of Attraction.*

The Basic Instinct of Love

Chapter Eight

Although many consider our basic instinct one of survival, we are ensured survival. We are eternal beings, so survival is imminent. Our basic instinct is one of love. This instinct has us protecting others and feeling sad when others are harmed. The *Law of Love*: love everything and everyone in the Universe, respect, love, light, truth, and peace. These are the virtues of natural law. The more you align with the *Law of Love*, the more power you will realize to create your future reality.

Notice that it is quite impossible for you to be filled with love, respect, light, truth, and peace and be negative and have destructive thoughts. The natural *Law of Love* makes positive thoughts much more powerful than negative thoughts. It's how we were meant to be. It's what we instinctively are. The law also prevents those who strive for abundance yet never consider benefits to others from ever achieving abundance. This selfishness may attract money, but it doesn't attract abundance.

We are to hate nothing – NOTHING! Not even what is perceived as bad because hatred is highly destructive, and destructive thoughts and beliefs will result in a future reality of destruction.

Have you ever seen great things come to those who are negative and think of lack and conformity regularly? No. The most significant results come from the most positive, creative people. You cannot get a healthy positive environment for yourself if your thoughts are predominantly negative, just as you cannot get an unhealthy negative environment if your thoughts are always positive and consistent with the greater good of all.

We have two general categories of emotions, those that feel good and those that feel bad. There's nothing in the natural *Law of Love* that should feel bad. When you feel good, you're working in alignment with the *Law of Love*. When you feel bad, you are not in alignment with the *Law of Love*. These feelings that feel bad are emotions based upon fear. When we have emotions that don't feel good, this is the spirit within us telling us we're off track and that we need to get back on track. Feelings that don't feel good are not meant to make our lives miserable. They're just meant to give us the feedback we need to change our course. We're not supposed to embrace bad feelings and allow them to linger.

Thoughts are the creative principle of the Universe and combine with other similar thoughts. The *Law of Growth* says that everything instinctively will grow. So negative thoughts will tend to grow more hostile, and positive thoughts will have a strong tendency to grow more pleasurable. Because the *Law of Love* is as strong as it is and our natural state of being, positive thoughts and positive things based on love grow much faster than negative thoughts and things. In either case, the *Law of Growth* will take thoughts into form and bring them into our reality.

The *Law of Attraction* always works this way, and your future reality depends upon your predominant mental attitude and habits, the words you say to yourself, and the pictures you've created in your mind.

> *"The most important words you will ever hear are*
> *the words you say to yourself. So, make them*
> *positive. Make them kind."*

> ~Marissa Peer

If you're thinking about lack and have negative thoughts all day, and then you decide to meditate for 20 minutes with positive thoughts, this will not likely bring you positive results because your predominant mental attitude and habits are negative. Your dominant mental attitude and habits must change, not just those you force yourself to have now and then but your everyday, all-the-time thoughts. Remember that the *most important words you'll hear are the words that you say to yourself* in thought.

Any thought that we persist in cannot fail to manifest. So thoughts of fear bring more fear. Thoughts of love for others bring you love. Thoughts that include hate of others bring you hate. Thoughts of abundance bring you abundance.

Thoughts of joy bring you joy. Thoughts of financial wealth bring you financial wealth.

Creating habits that naturally allow your thoughts to bring you what you desire is a tremendous investment. Additionally, since our natural state of being is instinctively in love, the thoughts that are positive and beneficial to all thrive.

You must see your negative feelings just as they were meant to be, as the negative feedback you need to know you are off track and to prompt you to change course. When you have a fearful or negative thought, your objective is to understand what is causing it. You can correct or change your thoughts to those that are more constructive. You must quickly and efficiently get rid of the negative thoughts. One way to eliminate a disempowering negative thought is to release it consciously.

Anytime a disempowering thought enters your mind, you eliminate it. You take a deep breath and release the negative. Focus on clearing your mind, just as taught in the meditation exercises.

The second method is to replace the disempowering negative thought with one that is positive and empowering. Most people find substituting another thought easier than eliminating a thought with no substitute. In other words, if you fill your mind with enough empowering thoughts, there won't be enough room to focus on the disempowering thought. Since the conscious mind has limited capabilities, unlike the subconscious, this method works and is a bit easier to manage.

Your imagination can do wonders for you in this regard. Close your eyes and imagine everything around you precisely the way you desire. Can you do this in your mind's eye? If you can, this is how you substitute your thoughts. You imagine it the way you desire.

The first step in mastering the *Law of Attraction* is recognizing that the real power comes from your inner voice or the spirit within you. You must realize your oneness with everyone in the Universe, your unity with the All-Powerful. Through your unity with the Universal Energy, your mind is the only creative principle within your control that is All-Powerful. Your creative thought, or imagination, ultimately takes form when in harmony with the natural *Law of Love* or all that is good. Until this realization occurs, you likely are trying to physically change your outer world versus changing it from the spirit within you that is united with everyone and everything and respects and loves all. The power we seek is spiritual, and it is what lies in the hearts of all things. It is the soul of the Universe.

The next step is to tap into this spiritual power, which will require you to think and act in a manner that allows you to receive this power, which ultimately means, practice, drill, and rehearse.

If you're not growing, you are dying. Thought is the origin of your growth and what prompts your conscious evolution. Everything you can create will first be created in your mind and later manifested into a reality.

Daydreaming is a form of mental dissipation, so don't mistake daydreaming for a form of imagination. Imagination is a form of creation. Imagination can create in your mind the perfect reality you desire. Using your imagination, unlike daydreaming, takes practice.

You must hold mental ideals of what you desire, and as you begin to attract bits and pieces of what you need to manifest your ideal, you constantly maintain in your mind's eye the desired result. Upon holding a mental ideal or perfect picture of what you desire, when opportunities present, you'll recognize them, receive them, and ultimately manifest the reality in direct proportion to your commitment to your perfect picture.

Imagination is the process that begins creating your heaven on earth. The power of imagination is how you can build a strong foundation of spiritual energy to support the vertical construction of your future. You can be protected from harm and live in abundance in all aspects of your life for eternity.

Meditation Exercise Eight

This week we'll take an object back to its origination. Use your analytical skills and look below the surface for its cause. Go as far back as possible and determine what prompted the physical object or activity.

Take your position and visualize something pleasurable. It could be your current home, the career you love, or anything that is pleasurable to you. Visualize this pleasantry in your mind's eye. Now go back to when you first saw your home or started the job you love.

- How did you come upon this thing, activity, or person?
- How did the object get there?
- How did the activity originate?
- How did you meet the person?
- When was it built?

Could you bring it back even further? In the case of an activity, when did it originate, and how? When was it designed, who designed it, and what were they thinking? If you're thinking about a relationship, how did you meet the person, and why is it that this person fits the bill? Even earlier, what materials are in the home? Is it a concrete foundation? Is it steel-reinforced? What about the change in construction styles? What influenced the styles? You get the idea. Take this so far back and visualize every step until you can't take it back any further.

It is probable that your home, career, or relationship originated with yourself or if taken back even further, by original thought. Regardless of what you choose, it originated as an individual thought, a group of people with a consensus of thought, or the creator's original thought. Isn't that correct? We likely find in the last analysis that our own thought or thoughts of society is responsible for this pleasurable experience and many other things seldom thought of.

You'll find exercises of this kind invaluable. Everything appears differently when the thought has been trained to look below the surface. The insignificant becomes significant, and the uninteresting becomes interesting. The things that were supposed to be unimportant are seen as the only vital things in existence.

The Perfect Spirit Within

Chapter 9

Most of our desires are focused on health, wealth, and love. The order of importance may vary, but most likely, all our desires fit within one of these categories. Love certainly is something that most can't live without, and that is love that gives us what we need to have fulfillment in all categories.

Without the love of self, it is quite challenging to prioritize your health. It is also difficult for others to trust you if you don't inherently show love for others, and trust is a crucial trait you must have to attract relationships that will lead to wealth.

In any regard, most will agree that fulfilling your health, wealth, and love desires will result in a joyous, abundant life. Learning to think correctly is how such a life can be delivered.

How do you think correctly? It's pretty simple. Your thinking must be consistent with truth. Think about it. If it's true, it's inevitable. The truth shall set us free, correct?

Most can predict an outcome when they know the result will be based on a universal truth, wouldn't you agree? Is the sun going to rise tomorrow? Of course, it is. Would you believe it if I told you that tomorrow would be different? Tomorrow the moon will rise instead of the sun. Would you believe me? Of course not.

You can't believe it because you know it's not true. Therefore, relying upon a result when the basis of the action is not true will result in an unexpected or undesirable outcome, and therefore we should avoid it.

What is true as it relates to the ideal state of being? What do you think as spiritual beings our true actual natural state of being is likely to be? Is it probable that our natural state of being is in harmony with the Divine? If you learn the truth about your natural state of being, you can have faith that anything you desire can be attained.

Let's explore the core universal truth of our higher power, which most consider perfect, strong, powerful, loving, and harmonious. Our higher power, the Infinite, the Universal Mind, God, Eternal Energy, the Divine, or whatever you call the Almighty, and which we are all united, is no less than perfect and within each of us. We are all one in spirit.

Whatever characteristics are possessed by our higher power, therefore, are also within each of us, within our Spirit. Spiritually we are perfect, strong, powerful, loving, and harmonious.

Thought is a creative spiritual activity. If you hold a thought in your mind, the perfect Spirit within you must deliver conditions and harmony with your thought. Thought is spiritual, and the Spirit is perfect and powerful. Therefore, thought must be in harmony with the circumstances delivered to you in the outer world.

If you desire financial wealth, understand that your Spirit is perfect and powerful and must deliver an outer world that is in harmony with your inner world. Therefore, you change your thoughts and concentrate on financial wealth for you and all. The perfect, powerful Spirit within will bring you into vibration with the forces that will deliver to you the circumstances that match your thoughts and manifest financial wealth. This is the 'truth' about the All-Powerful Spirit within you.

Your imagination is the key to your spiritual power. Your imagination is the creative expression of your inner world. Seeing things in your mind's eye is very different from seeing things with your eyes. Your eyes see things only in your outer world, and the outer world is only the result of your inner world. Your inner world is the cause or action that creates the outer world. Creative visualization in your mind's eye allows your powerful Spirit to set the spiritual forces in motion that bring you into vibration with what you focus on giving you the result in your outer world.

Your greatest spiritual truth is that you're perfect, strong, loving, and harmonious Spirit is united with the Infinite and always brings you into vibration with what you focus on. It is guaranteed.

Many medical miracles have been documented that show the power of thought. Thought can change the result associated with what most would consider incurable. How does this happen? Time and time again, it is explained by faith. The individual believes so strongly in the Infinite Power that they will change the outcome simply by willing it to be.

The Infinite is All-Powerful and can eliminate all fear, lack, and pain and attract all pleasure, abundance, and joy.

Time and time again, those who have been fortunate to have this faith cure their supposedly incurable disease by creating a vision and affirmations focusing upon what is most needed, claiming it repeatedly.

This behavior is a choice that can be learned and applied to any situation you desire. You are to create a vision statement opposite to the current undesirable situation. Substitute the disempowering thought with the empowering thought for you and all and think it repeatedly.

Whenever you send out thoughts that are good for all, they return multiplied. For example, 'I am perfect, strong, powerful, loving, and harmonious' can easily be said, 'we are all perfect, strong, powerful, loving, and harmonious.' Rotating these two vision statements is oh-so powerful.

Now how are you going to ensure that you think only empowering thoughts? You must eliminate negative, disempowering thoughts as they enter your mind. This is easier said than done. At first, you'll find that disempowering thoughts pop into your head regularly. You must forget... eliminate... terminate them!

Tony Robbins used to hold a seminar. I'm not sure if he still does this, but one of the exercises the participants perform is his famous fire walk, where the participants control their thoughts to the point that they believe that they are walking on 'cool moss' versus 'hot coals.' It sounds challenging, especially when you know it's not true.

If you focus 100% on something, no other thought can get into your consciousness. Therefore, the seed that you planted in your subconscious mind, that the coals were cool moss, grows and expands sufficiently that you can walk over hot coals without burning your feet or feeling the heat of the coals.

You can apply this to any unproductive thought. Your new empowering thoughts can smother the disempowering thoughts and begin to grow. When you get a disempowering thought, take the opposite empowering thought and create a powerful vision statement. Memorize this powerful vision statement and repeat it as often as possible. Repeat it regularly over and over again. Concentrate the thought so intensely that the negative, disempowering thought gets smothered and dies, leaving fertile ground for your empowering thought to grow and eventually become a solid belief within your subconscious.

When you concentrate on thought this way, the effect is as apparent as a magnifying glass focusing on the sun's power.

You must eliminate or avoid the negativity of others as well. When others present negativity, focus on the bright side of the issuer situation, and when appropriate, change the subject to something pleasant. Don't be afraid to remove yourself from negative people or situations when your presence isn't necessary. Ensure that your thoughts get back on track with positivity.

Additionally, ensure that your predominant mental attitude is consistent with the perfect, powerful, loving, strong, harmonious Spirit within you. You can't think all day negatively and then believe that one concentrated positive thought will work.

Ultimately, your thoughts are the actions you take that create the result or conditions in your outer world. Thoughts are the cause, and your outer world reality is the effect. This is the *Law of Cause and Effect*, the *Law of Attraction*, and is believed by many to be the origin of good and evil.

The perfect Spirit within you must relate your outer world conditions to your thoughts. Therefore, if your thoughts are perfect, strong, powerful, loving, and harmonious, the conditions in your outer world will match those thoughts. If your thoughts are faulty, weak, violent, hateful, and hostile, the conditions in your outer world will also match those thoughts.

Good and evil... your positive, loving thoughts are in harmony with the Universe, and your negative thoughts are your devil.

"As thy faith is, so be it unto thee."

Either way you look at it, the *Law of Attraction* or the power of prayer works.

Meditation Exercise Nine

Visualize a 500-year-old oak tree. Remember when the earth's ground in which the tree now stands was bare. See the tiny plant burst through the soil. It is now a living thing, something alive and beginning to search for the meaning of sustaining life. Plant an acorn in a spot, water it, care for it, and ensure that it gets the direct rays of the morning sun.

Now see yourself at the location in which the tree now stands. See the roots penetrating the earth, watch them shoot out in all directions, and remember that they are living cells dividing and subdividing and will soon number millions. Remember that each cell is intelligent and knows what it wants and how to get it. See the stem shoot forward and upward. Watch it divide and form branches. See how perfect and symmetrical each branch is formed. See the leaves begin to develop, and as you watch, a giant beauty of nature unfolds perfectly. If you concentrate intently, you will become conscious of its smell. You can smell the leaves as the breeze gently sways the beautiful creation you have visualized.

Now see the branches divide and subdivide as the magnificent tree overwhelms the acorns beneath it. See the sunset and winter come. Watch the leaves turn colors and fall to the ground as this magnificent giant looks vulnerable to the world. See springtime buds begin to form as life begins to be evident and the breath of life consumes the tree, while you know that every intelligent cell knows how to attract what it needs to live in perfect harmony with the Universe.

When you can make your vision clear and complete, you will be able to enter into the spirit of a thing. It will become very real to you. You will be learning to concentrate. The process is the same whether you are focused on health, a grand oak tree, an ideal, a complicated business proposition, or any other life problem.

Nothing Happens by Accident

Chapter Ten

Nothing happens by accident. There is a cause for all things that occur. You co-create your future when you learn how to control any situation by bringing appropriate causes into action. You can continue to live your life, allowing unknown causes to create effects and be governed by your feelings and emotions as they happen without conscious interpretation, or you can decide to design your destiny.

You can no longer make excuses or blame anything or anyone else for your lack of results or the unfavorable circumstance that you find yourself in. You will know that the Universe has responded to your command.

The natural laws of the Universe govern cause and effect. Cause and effect occur in our inner and outer worlds, based on this natural law itself and the Spiritual Power, with unlimited resources, behind the law.

We live in an abundant Universe. All you must do is look around. Nature is bountiful and excessive in everything. Everything from plants to animals reproduces abundantly and continues to create and recreate in excess. No conservation efforts occur naturally in anything that is created.

Yet, the dirt and ground on our earth are lifeless and cannot create life. Never has the soil and land created life, and they never will. Not a single atom of our mineral world can ever create life. No evidence anywhere in the Universe proves that life has ever or ever will be created by anything other than life itself. At the point of life's first existence, science has no explanation.

When you plant an acorn, and the roots begin to grow, they reach into the mineral world, and there is life. The soil is useless without the acorn from a living tree. Once the acorn is seated in this lifeless soil, a suitable environment miraculously develops as the *Law of Growth* begins to take effect. The acorn sprouts the roots that create life into the otherwise dead soil. As the acorn's roots grow, we see the first sign of life being created as it breaks through the earth's crust, and an oak tree unfolds before us.

Similarly, the individual is lifeless. It is the Spirit that gives us life. Universal Energy reaches down into the human mind and gives it life; our thoughts link us to the Infinite. Think about it. It's not as if we can reach up and grab some spirit and put it into a stuffed animal to become alive. Without the Spirit, our bodies alone are lifeless.

When you plant a thought in the Universal Mind, the roots begin to grow. The thought is given life, and then amazingly results begin as the *Law of Growth* takes effect. As the thought continues to grow in the Universal Mind, we begin to see the first sign as the creation breaks through the barrier between the inner and outer worlds as the evidence of your thought begins to unfold in your outer world.

Thought is a powerful form of dynamic energy that aligns with its object and brings it from the inner world to the outer world. This is the law in which all things are created.

They are first created in thought and then realized in our physical world by the power of the Infinite.

Now make sure to distinguish creation from evolution. Creation is quite different. Creation is something new, bringing into the physical world something that currently does not exist. Evolution is a change involving things that already exist in the physical world.

You have the power within to co-create. You think it and then allow the Infinite to create it. 'Decree a thing, and it shall be established unto thee.' However, this power does not form the physical being that you are. It is the power of the Creator. As Jesus said, *"It is not I that doeth the works, but the Father that dwelleth within me, He doeth the work."*

You don't have the power to influence universal laws or to assist these laws in bringing about creation. You comply with the law, and the All-Powerful will bring about the result of your thoughts.

Your objective must be to imagine the perfect picture of the desired result. Don't worry whether you have the intelligence or a well-thought-out, detailed plan to bring about your desires. The Infinite with unlimited resources can be depended upon to find the best way to bring about the desired result, and you will be presented with what is needed when needed.

Electricity, cellular service, satellites, and radio waves are all energies, currents, or vibrations. They are invisible, yet they each have laws that apply to them that make them work. You may not understand how these laws work, but that's irrelevant to those who desire to benefit from them. Your objective is to learn how to operate within the laws that govern these objects.

How do you live in harmony with a law unless you know what the law is? Most of our fabulous inventions required observations and trial and error. Over and over again they test this and that, and eventually, the results showed clearly that the invention found a way to operate in harmony with the laws that govern these invisible powers.

Likewise, how do you know how to operate in harmony with natural, universal laws that bring about desired results and our outer world? Over and over again, test this and that, and eventually, the result clearly shows how to operate in harmony with the laws that govern the invisible spiritual power. Similarly, it is through observations and trial and error.

For more than 2000 years, great teachers have shared their observations. Nature has expressed itself constantly, and it is readily observable by all. Where there's growth, there must be life. This is indisputable. Where there is life, there must be harmony so that everything that has life constantly attains the conditions necessary for its complete expression.

Consider the waters of the ocean and the forest when left undisturbed. Life attracts the conditions and supply of whatever is needed to be abundant and fully expressed. Life seeks harmony to flourish.

When considering radio waves, harmony forms a circuit and allows the music being broadcasted to be heard miles away from the broadcast. You don't hear any music when the circuit is not formed; the result could be static or nothing.

Like the laws that allow radio waves to work, when your thoughts are in harmony with the principles of nature or the Infinite Mind, you operate in vibrational alignment, and the circuit is formed. You receive the benefits of what is being broadcast. When the circuit is not formed, or when you're not operating within these principles, you don't receive the benefit of what's being broadcast.

If your thoughts are not harmonious with the Infinite, you will not create the circuit, and your thoughts will remain with you. Thoughts that remain with you in this regard are not healthy and bring about worry, doubt, and fear.

As a result, the solar plexus contracts and cannot radiate the energy to your muscles and nerves, which ultimately is unhealthy.

Therefore, your creative thoughts must be harmonious to create abundance in the outer world. Thoughts that are not harmonious are destructive to you unless eliminated.

"Never talk defeat. Use words like hope, belief, faith, and victory."

~Norman Vincent Peale

Ultimately, all harmonious conditions result from the power that comes from within. You develop power by practice. The more you consciously control your thoughts to think only harmonious thoughts consistent with the natural principles of the Infinite, the more power you develop and the more you can co-create everything you desire. The objective, then, would be to develop power.

Meditation Exercise Ten

Abundance won't drop in your lap out of the clear blue sky. You must act. The conscious realization of the *Law of Action* and operating in harmony with the Infinite will materialize your desire.

> *"It's not enough to know what to do; you must do what you know."*

> ~Tammy Gallagher

Take your position and select a blank space on the wall, and mentally draw a black horizontal line about 6 inches long. See the line as plainly as though it were painted on the wall. Now mentally draw two vertical lines connecting with the horizontal line at both ends. Now draw another horizontal line connecting the ends of the two vertical lines. You now have a rectangle. Make all of the lines the same length. You now have a square.

See the square perfectly. Then draw a large circle within the square. Place a point in the center of the circle and draw the point toward you about 10 inches. You should be visualizing a cone on a square base.

Change the color of your lines from black to white, then red, then yellow. Now change the color of the entire drawing to orange. Make it three dimensional and rotate the cone so you can picture it standing on its base. If you can do this, you are making excellent progress and will soon be able to concentrate on any situation you desire.

Faith Will Deliver Miracles

Chapter 11

We all know people who have achieved amazing things. They have changed everything in their lives, and mainly they have changed themselves. We may call this a fantastic transformation or a miracle. However, all required to bring about this level of achievement, or transformation, is an understanding of the truth of the power of prayer or the *Law of Attraction*.

This powerful law eliminates the uncertainty in our lives and provides us with consistent predetermined results every time. You are fortunate to be here in this place and time in which this power within you has been recognized and realized throughout every civilized nation in the world. Many are attaining results through a process that they don't even understand.

If you were to eliminate free will or your ability to choose consciously, what results would you realize with the *Law of attraction*? And why do opposites attract? How does all this fit together?

Let's ponder the Universe itself. By what means is everything in the Universe kept together? When we consider magnetic forces, opposites attract, and like forces need their distance from each other. This distance among like forces seems to keep stars, and other planets at a sufficient distance from each other and, in turn, keeps the Universe in harmony.

On the other hand, we tend to see opposites in people attract. We see it regularly in business relationships or personal relationships. People with nothing in common seem to develop better relationships than those with much. Why is that so?

In a business partnership, if both partners bring precisely the same personal attributes and strengths, one of the partners would be unnecessary. We tend to have demands for what we do not possess. This is the *Law of Supply and Demand.*

A disturbance is observed in the motion of Uranus, and another star is needed to keep the solar system in place. Neptune arrives precisely on schedule. Where there is a demand, supply is created. This well-defined need or demand receives its solution by natural law. It attracts what it needs almost instantly.

In this example, no thought occurs. Its intelligence results in precisely the perfect outcome every time. With us, however, we can choose what we desire and therefore create different results. Our choices tend to focus on something that will complete us somehow. We have a demand, and the unlimited resources of the Infinite provides the supply.

The choice is a result of a thought that is active and creative. Through our thoughts, things can be created, and this creation in our mind ultimately creates here on earth. Once your thoughts break through you, becoming a part of your subconscious and therefore united with the Infinite, they pass from truth to truth in the eternal light, where all of this is, was, or ever shall be, is harmonized.

From your silent reflection and contemplation, you become inspired. This inspiration comes from the Divine source and the inception of a new creation, or demand, in your mind. The Divine is creative and intelligent, superior to all other external forces, and therefore can understand and possess every element of your outer world.

Thought is the most remarkable, most powerful finding of all time. This intelligent, creative power takes your ideas and makes them live in the outer world. Jesus said, *"What things soever you desire, when ye pray, believe that ye receive them, and ye shall have them."*

Those who have mastered this understanding seem to have everything come to them so easily. They never appear to have difficulty, and it's as if everything goes right for them all the time. They always seem happy and live perfectly with themselves and the Universe.

At the moment you believe that your desire has already been fulfilled, you are planting the seed of thought of absolute perfection, eliminating any limitations. The seed, if left undisturbed, will germinate in your outer world reality as the forces are set in motion to bring it about in your outer world.

Technology has given us the ability to connect with millions today. To be able to pass on this simple but powerful truth to so many more than ever before, placing us in a unique point in time that is more wonderful than ever dreamed of by most. Regardless of your perspective, there is the same underlying truth.

- Jesus said, "*Believe that ye receive, and ye shall receive.*"
- Paul said, "*Faith is the substance of things hoped for, the evidence of things not seen.*"
- The *Law of Attraction* is the law by which thought correlates with its object.

All three statements result in the same outcome or the exact cause and effect. They are just different perspectives of the same truth. This does not mean there is no truth to any of these statements. It simply better defines it and shows how it is being held concerning our needs and becoming more understood. Truth's completeness requires a variety of perspectives and is not limited to only one perspective.

Which perspective resonates with you is irrelevant. They all mean that when you learn to impress upon the Universal Mind the image showing that your desire is already an existing fact, and you do so without doubt or reservation, you have mastered the power of your creative thought. You will know how to use the power to solve every problem you ever have, and the Universe will apply this to your demand. You will have realized the marvelous gift given to all by God.

Meditation Exercise Eleven

In this exercise, you are going to do something a little different. Take your meditation position, and still your body and mind, then relax your body and mind. Inhibit thought.

Now concentrate on the following quote from the Bible: "Whatsoever things ye desire, when ye pray, believe that you receive them and ye shall have them."

Make sure that there are no limitations when you focus on this statement. 'Whatsoever things' is obvious and implies that the only limitation is those we place upon ourselves through our thoughts. Remember that faith is the essence of things hoped for, the evidence of things not seen.

God's Gift of

Thought

Chapter Twelve

God's gift of thought, and therefore, the power to create, has been given to everyone and is unlimited. Creation is our Divine purpose. The creative power we all have within us due to our unity with the Infinite gives us independence and freedom.

You can co-create an ideal situation in your business life, at home, and with your friends and acquaintances without regard to resources or costs. The omnipotence of your thought will draw upon the unlimited resources of the Infinite, and all that you need will be at your command.

There are three steps to ensure that you attract what you desire.

- It is essential first to understand the power of the Spirit within.
- You must then have the courage to act.
- Finally, you must have faith to allow it to happen.

"To one who has faith, no explanation is necessary.
To one without faith, no explanation is possible."

~Saint Thomas Aquinas

All power comes from the Spirit within, and through tranquility and the stillness of the mind, you unite with the omnipotent power of the Infinite through your subconscious mind.

If you desire power, wisdom, or permanent success in any regard, you will find it only within. Understand that only in absolute silence may you come in contact with Divinity. A silent, still mind is not an easy feat, so persistent practice is necessary, and your reward will lead to power. This power will increase as you become more proficient in using it. More importantly, the power is permanent and carries no adverse conditions, providing long-term results when used.

Everything that is created is created in consciousness first. By governing your thoughts today, you shape your future events and environment. Feelings of love united with your desires, and the proper education, is the most potent combination with the *Law of Attraction.*

To some, this concept is entirely different from what they've been taught, and it isn't easy to comprehend. Why is it so difficult to accept a new idea? Change seems painful as we venture into something we've never experienced before. In most cases, we are conditioned, and our minds cannot comprehend something entirely new until we are prepared to receive it.

You must create the necessary brain cells through a concentrated focus, which will be ready to receive the omnipotence of the *Law of Attraction*, enabling you to comprehend the unlimited power that's within you. You must become a vibrational match.

Once you have come to a proper understanding of the power within you, then you must act upon it. It is evident that we attract what we focus on, yet somehow, we still have doubts, fears, anxiety, or worry. Like all negative thoughts, these disempowering thoughts stay with us and keep our desires further away from us. All disempowering thoughts are not in harmony with the Universe and remain with you. They cannot be united with the Universal Mind. These disempowering thoughts linger with you, and ultimately, you reap what you sow.

Therefore, if you think disempowering thoughts more often than empowering, you keep pushing away those things you desire.

A thought will correlate with its object and will be delivered to you in the physical world as long as your thoughts are in harmony with the Universe. Being in harmony with the Universe requires that your thoughts carry truth. This harmony is what allows the *Law of Growth* to manifest your thoughts.

The *Law of Attraction*, or the power of prayer, gives thought the power to correlate with its object and, ultimately, to master every adverse condition you face. Love conveys life into thought. Any thought that is permeated with love is unconquerable. The Infinite is intelligent. But it is also energy. This energy gets its vitality from the feelings generated by love and is the force that brings electrons together by the *Law of Attraction* so that they can form atoms. The atoms are energized together and form molecules, which take the form of the material objects of our desire.

The feelings generated by love are the creative force that sparks the chain of events that ultimately results in your desires being manifested. The combination of thought brought alive with love creates the unconquerable cause that the *Law of Attraction* has a constructive effect.

All universal laws are unconquerable: electricity, radio waves, cellular signals, and gravitation. Cellular phones are common today. However, when you're talking on a cellular phone and your phone call is dropped, you don't blame the natural law that allows cellular signals to operate cell phones. You know that something is blocking the signal. Similarly, you cannot blame the *Law of Attraction* for not delivering your desired result. You cannot blame God for not answering your prayers. Instead, we must look at the aspects within our control. It will likely be something as simple as needing to understand the application that caused the lack of our desires to manifest.

Define your ideal picture or vision clearly. The end picture must be precisely concluded. You don't have to worry about the details associated with how you get to the result or perfect picture. The Universe has the resources to fill in the gaps more adequately than you do, so focus on the detailed result. Not only must it be defined, but it must be consistent. Changing your perfect picture weekly will not create the subconscious realization of your desire.

An architect started working on plans, and the picture in his mind's eye was of a two-story contemporary home but the next week he decided to change it to a traditional ranch. The following week, he thought he might be better with a Tudor-style home. When do you think he'll finish the plans, and what would the end plan look like? Would you have a clear set of plans by the end of the third week? It's not likely. Therefore, plans can only begin to be finalized with a clear result, or the things you desire will be continually delayed and fragmented.

You do this consistently if you direct concentrated thought without other thoughts interrupting you. In that case, you will be delivered powerful results, and your desires will be created in your reality.

Meditation Exercise Twelve

In your usual meditation place, relax and let go, mentally and physically. Always do this and never try to do any mental work under pressure. Ensure that there are no tense muscles or nerves and that you are entirely comfortable. Now realize your unity with the Infinite. Get in touch with this power. Come into deep and vital understanding, appreciation, and realization that your ability to think is your ability to act upon the Universal Mind and bring it into manifestation.

Realize that the power of the Divine will meet every requirement and that you already have the same potential ability that any individual has ever had or ever will have because each of us is an expression or manifestation of the Infinite. All of us are parts of the whole. There is no difference in kind or quality. The only difference is of degree.

The Father and I Are One

Chapter Thirteen

Some people hold extraordinary spiritual capabilities yet are often brushed off and not accepted as people with true spiritual power. Without scientific proof, many in our society find it difficult to believe anything. However, inductive reasoning has been used repeatedly to prove the truth. Yet, resistance is still related to the spiritual power of thought.

Some conclude that there are people who hold supernatural powers for which there is no explanation. However, just because there's no explanation doesn't mean there's no truth to these powers. Inductive reasoning is convincing that every phenomenon results from a definite cause and natural law or principle that operates with precision every time.

The inductive science of careful repeated observations in many circumstances concludes that there are many occurrences whose internal operations we don't understand. Yet, the principle by which the occurrence operates is consistent and reliable.

Some believe that these unexplained occurrences are things we should leave alone. But if you look throughout time, many of our advances and knowledge have been a direct result of someone boldly questioning what was perceived by some as 'forbidden ground.'

Inductive science confirms that thought is spiritual, creative, and powerful. Thought, when consciously directed toward empowering beliefs of faith, courage, and enthusiasm, is the spiritual power tool we all have been given to achieve our desires.

Our predominant mental attitude sets the stage for every condition we experience. Empowering thoughts will result in pleasant circumstances, just as disempowering thoughts will result in unpleasant circumstances. If you fear tragedy and therefore focus on it, tragedy will result. If your predominant thoughts are upon joy, joy will be delivered.

One challenge is that many things we focus on don't give us the satisfaction we thought they would once we get them, or they provide only temporary satisfaction. The Universal Mind does not decide whether what we focus on is going to satisfy us or not; it simply delivers to us that in which we believe.

Ask yourself, what do you want in life? What do you want? Don't answer this from a micro perspective. Answer it from a macro perspective.

It is likely that everyone, yes, everyone, wants the same thing, and that's happiness and harmony. If we're happy, we have everything we want or need, and if we're happy, we have more of ourselves to give.

"Remember, happiness doesn't depend upon who you are or what you have; it depends solely upon what you think."

~Dale Carnegie

To be happy, most of us would agree that we would want to be in excellent health, have harmonious, exciting, loving relationships, and have an abundant supply of all the material items we desire. If you throw away all limitations, you want the best of everything.

Would you be happy if you were healthy, had great, harmonious, exciting, loving relationships, and had an abundant supply of all the material items you desire?

Jesus said, "*Father and I are one.*" The Father is our creator and the original substance from which all things are made. The concept of the Father within you has been taught for over 2000 years. It is the core belief of almost every system of philosophy or religion and can pretty much be considered truth among the majority.

So how is it that we get the tangible results of health, love, and wealth that the Father, our Creator within us, is capable of delivering to anyone and everyone? Through our creative power of thought. Thought is our spiritual power. It is the explanation for every condition or circumstance. The day of the dreamer has come.

Recognize that it's not enough to know what to do. You must do what you know. Nothing is ever accomplished by knowledge alone. The phrase 'knowledge is power' is not entirely accurate. The improved statement is that 'knowledge and thought put into action is power.' Thoughts are the cause, and your circumstance is the effect. Empowering thoughts of courage, love, health, or caring for others set causes in motion to deliver the desired effects. It's as simple as giving mentally.

An unhappy thought cannot exist in a happy state of mind. Staying focused on the thoughts that make you feel happy and good is necessary to place the *Law of Attraction* into action in your life. Remember also that you are a finite being with limited resources. Yet the Infinite is limitless with infinite resources. You are to therefore create a mental image of your perfect outcome without predetermining the path on which you will get there. Allow the Infinite's unlimited resources to present the proper path.

"When one has made one's demands upon the
universal, one must be ready for surprises.

Everything may seem to be going wrong when in reality, it is going right."

~Florence Scovel Shin

By detaching yourself from the path to your perfect outcome, you allow the Infinite resources to find the most efficient path. This may, at times, present you with what appears to be chaos or unexpected circumstances. However, have faith that the path will deliver your desired outcome. Listen to your inner voice and focus on your desired outcome; your feelings will guide you appropriately.

When creating your perfect picture in your mind's eye, also remember that you must focus on how you want to feel in the perfect situation. Remaining focused on how you feel always allows the Infinite to fill in the gaps with the most efficient and effective means, to deliver the conditions and feelings you created in your mind.

Through the *Law of Causation*, dreamers bring their desires into their reality. When you begin to unconsciously come into the understanding of this tremendous realization that you are part of the whole, and the spirit within you is truly united with the Divine, that you are one with the creator and the same in quality and kind, that 'The Father and I are one,' then you will understand the transcendental possibilities that are at your command.

Meditation Exercise Thirteen

This lesson is simple but powerful. Take your position and still your body and mind, then relax your body and mind, and inhibit thought. Now, recognize that you are a part of the whole and that 'The Father and I are one,' is a true statement for you. A part must be the same in kind and quality as the whole, with the only difference being degree. You can become a vessel by which the Infinite can answer your prayers and bring about the realization of your desire.

The Uncertainty Principle

Chapter Fourteen

You have learned that your outer world is controlled by an unexplainable power universally accepted as God and that we are all united with this All-Powerful source. You'll also learn that thought is a creative spiritual process, and it is powerful. This power, however, doesn't originate within you but from the Infinite channeled through you.

You understand that the conscious and subconscious minds work together as one mind. The conscious mind directs the subconscious by creating beliefs for the subconscious to act upon. The subconscious mind is united with the Universal Mind, and this unity allows us access to all power and the unlimited resources of the Infinite.

How does all of this relate to science or, better yet, to physics? The answer will amaze you. When I first learned of the uncertainty principle in 2007, it seemed outrageous to comprehend.

Let's first review the makeup of all matter. Matter comprises molecules, which are made of atoms and electrons. In physics, an uncertainty principle concludes that there is no guarantee about the pattern of electrons. When looking at the probability that an electron will arrive in a given circumstance, the conclusion is that it is impossible to predict precisely what will happen.[12] Only the odds can be predicted. Physics has given up on finding a solution to this unpredictability. Yes! Physics has given up. Science has given up.

Even more mind boggling is that the predictability of electrons changes when electrons are observed.[12] It is suspected that it will be impossible ever to find the answer to this mystery and accept it as nature really is. Some physicists believe that electrons have and internal variable that science isn't aware of, possibly that is why it cannot be predicted. They believe that this internal variable is thought—human thought.

Yes, thought could be the variable that will change the outcome of how electrons respond. Electrons don't form atoms, which won't form molecules and will not unite with other molecules to form matter if it weren't for thought. Without thought intervention, electrons would remain without assembling into atoms and molecules. How can this be? What happens to the electrons when we're not observing them if they don't assemble into atoms, which ultimately make up matter?

The Infinite Energy, in which we are all united, is also united with electrons, and this may very well be the cause behind electrons assembling when thought is present versus when it is not. This is mind-boggling to me. For example, the electrons of a ball are not in the shape of a ball unless there is an observer who knows it's a ball. Knowing it's a ball is gained through the individual's unity with the Universal Mind. This explains how we manifest our thoughts and beliefs into reality. Electrons have the same potential speed as all other cosmic energy, such as light, electricity, and thought. Light travels about 186,000 miles a second. In essence, electrons travel similarly to the speed of light and likely faster. They can assemble almost instantaneously when they are within our site. And, due to our limited capabilities, and the speed in which electrons travel, this assemblage happens without us being able to see it happening.

Electrons fill all space and are ultimately everywhere, even what appears to be empty. So, in essence, electrons make up everything in our physical world and could be considered the Universal Substance from which all material things are made. If electrons are the Universal Substance, then the Infinite permeates electrons.

All things originate in thought and appear physically due to thought-directing electrons. That same power can also eliminate things. It is thought that gives all matter forms in our physical world.

For every effect, there is a cause. If we follow the trail of every effect backward in time, we will find the creative thought from which the effect grew.

Let's look at how all of this relates to our bodies. Every part of our body is made up of cells. Some of these cells rely upon each other, and some are independent. All cells have enough intelligence to perform all functions they are required to perform. All cells are intelligent enough to ensure their future existence. These cells choose what they need and what they don't need. Each cell is born, reproduces itself, dies, and is absorbed. Life itself requires the continuous renewal of these cells.

The mind of our cells is that of our subconscious mind. Cells act without thought or conscious knowledge and are responsive to the will of our conscious mind. This is the explanation for metaphysical healing. The power of a belief in the subconscious mind also provides the manifestations as it relates to our bodies.

God is Infinite, has unlimited resources, and is omnipresent. Therefore, we must be an expression or manifestation of this All-Powerful Mind. Our subconscious, which gives intelligence to our cells, is united with God's mind, the Universal Mind, which is united with intelligence and electrons, and so on. The All-Powerful Universal Mind is in everything and everyone; the resources available to us through this unity are limitless, and what gives creative thought so much power.

Your subconscious mind is the link between your conscious mind, your mental world, and the Universal Mind of the spiritual world. You have direct access to God or the Infinite. It is, therefore, evident that no limits can be placed upon the power of thought when in alignment with all that is good. Do you realize that recognizing this fact places you in touch with Omnipotence?

Thoughts, faith, alignment with the Universe, and all that is good will manifest every time. Thoughts that are disempowering and not aligned with the Universe will stay with you and can never enter the vibrational force of Eternal Energy. They will deliver negative results. Understanding this principle explains the power of prayer.

We need to think and pray correctly. Thought creates our beliefs, and this is the only reality that will ever manifest. Thoughts with faith, are like prayers with faith. Thoughts will only materialize with faith. Conditions and circumstances in our physical world are outward manifestations of thought. If we change our thoughts and beliefs, we change our material conditions, as conditions must be in harmony with their creator. And our thoughts unite with the Universal Mind through our subconscious mind.

When our thoughts have faith and conviction and are in harmony with the Infinite, we will achieve what we believe and can conceive every time.

So here is the secret: thought must be empowering, focused, defined, consistent, and aligned with the universal good. You can't spend a lifetime thinking negatively and expect 20 to 30 minutes a day of positive thinking to work overnight.

If you decide today to be disciplined, you must ensure that nothing interferes with your decision. This decision to change the way you think is the decision to change your life. Not only will you bring about benefits and material things, but you will also experience more love and physical health.

Who you are is a reflection of your thoughts and beliefs. It's your character, your environment, and even your appearance. To change who you are, you must change how you think.

Meditation Exercise Fourteen

In your position, as usual, completely relax. Concentrate on harmony, which means with all that the word implies. Concentrate so profoundly and intently that you will be conscious of nothing but harmony. Remember, we learn by doing. Reading these lessons is only the start. Action and practical application are what will create results.

The Importance of Words

Chapter Fifteen

Universal laws, when understood and applied properly, consistently work to your advantage and are always in process.

The Eternal Energy that sets the forces in motion to deliver what you desire and picture perfectly in your mind's eye needs your imagination and for you to operate in harmony with all that is good. Anytime you're not in harmony with the Infinite, you are either refusing to release something you no longer need or refusing to accept something you require.

We grow by exchanging the old for the new, the good for the improved. You can't get what you lack if you keep holding on to what you have.

Your ability to take from each experience only what you need while releasing what you don't need will determine the degree of harmony and happiness you'll attain.

As you expand your visions and ascend to greater levels of awareness, you improve your ability to understand your true desires and what you are to focus on to attract what you need to attain them.

Everything that happens to you occurs for your benefit. When the things that come to you are not the things that you want, then it's because you somehow haven't learned what you are supposed to do, and until you do, you will continue to have circumstances that you don't want.

To grow, you must become in consciousness what you want to attract. You must behave the way you want to be treated. You know the golden rule. 'Do unto others as you would have them do unto you.'

Ultimately, understanding the universal laws and applying them will ensure your desired outcome and happiness. The universal *Law of Reciprocity* states that you benefit in an expanded proportion to your effort. The effort you put forth now to understand universal laws will reward you with happiness in the future.

For your thoughts to have vitality or life, they must be drenched with love. Since love is a strong emotion, your thoughts must be guided by reason but filled with love. Love gives thoughts life and allows it to grow. The *Law of Attraction* doesn't work for thoughts that aren't filled with love.

Thought expresses itself in physical form, and all your thoughts lead to some effect. This makes it evident that you can think only positive thoughts and thoughts consistent with your true desires.

Thoughts are often expressed through the words we use, even when the words are in our heads. It is essential that you use only empowering words that align with the abundance you desire in your life, as your mind's eye visualizes by mirroring the words you use.

The correct choice of words will lead to improved pictures in your mind. The more you clearly define these things through proper words, the more clearly defined your pictures become.

Our ability to formulate thought through words makes us different from any other animal that walks the earth. Words create mental pictures that are eternal and allow us to pass on eternal knowledge and document history. They allow us to visualize our future to influence its outcome. Words allow us to create visions and dreams of the future.

We have been able to record the greatest thinkers and writers of all time, and this record is that of Universal Thought taking form in the minds of individuals. These individuals act as messengers.

Words are a form of thought that express themselves in form. The unity of all harmonious thought or Universal Thought is the Creator, and this thought manifests through individual thought. Therefore, we must choose our words carefully.

Words are a means by which the Universe gives us access to unlimited resources. When in alignment with all that is good, our word expressions enter the well-being stream and materialize.

Principles are the backbone of mathematics, health, light, truth, and abundance. It is no surprise that principle exists in thought. A thought with vitality has principle, and vitality gives thought power.

We know this is true because we are sure of the result when we apply the principle correctly. For example, the darkness is no longer there when we shine light in a room. When we tell the truth, we can't be dishonest.

These are indisputable facts. Just like vital thoughts contain principle, life, and lives by the *Law of Growth*. Vital thoughts take root and smother negative thoughts. Negative thoughts, by their nature, contain no vitality.

This fact, which continues to show true every time, enables you to destroy all negativism, lack, and limitation. If you understand the creative power of thought, you master your destiny.

The appearance of a given amount of energy anywhere means the disappearance of the same amount somewhere else. We can receive only what we give away. Therefore, we don't want to give others what we don't wish upon ourselves.

Meditation Exercise Fifteen

Insight is something that we attain and develop. It is essential to any outstanding achievement and is obtained through silent reflection and concentration. It allows us to be prepared for obstacles before we ever experience them. Insight paves the road in front of us that permits us to develop plans in the right direction.

This exercise has you concentrating on insight. In meditation, focus the thought on the fact that knowing the creative power of thought is significantly more potent than possessing the ability to think. Let the thought dwell on the fact that knowledge does not apply itself. Your actions are not governed by knowledge but by custom, precedent, and habit. The only way you can get yourself to apply knowledge is by a determined conscious effort.

Call to mind the fact that unused knowledge is forgotten and that the value of the information is in applying the principle. Continue this line of thought until you gain sufficient insight to formulate a definite program for applying this principle to a particular circumstance, challenge, or opportunity.

Specifically, concentrate on a goal that you already have the knowledge needed. You've had this knowledge, but have you applied it? Get creative and concentrate on using this knowledge and putting it into action through the conscious creative effort of thought. It is not enough to know what to do; you must do what you know.

What is Your Purpose?

Chapter Sixteen

Most agree that wealth, health, and love are the three predominant characteristics that, when acquired, can add to your happiness and success in your outer world.

Financial wealth can be described as the possession of things that provide exchange value. It is an effect, however, not a cause. It is the result of your actions and provides a means for you to continue to create. It should never be desired as an end but as a means of accomplishing your desires.

Success is not financial wealth but a higher ideal with a definite purpose. To truly attain financial wealth, you must have a definite purpose or ideal that benefits more than just you. With a definite purpose, the means and abundance will be provided.

Spend some time right now and ask this question of yourself. What is your definite purpose or ideal? Consider what you do every day that benefits others. If you are unsatisfied with your answer, concentrate on what you want to bring to others. How can you maximize benefits to all in what you enjoy doing every day?

Great fortune comes from spiritual power. There are many clear examples. Think of those whom you consider your heroes in life. Were they given everything? Were they given anything of significance? Did they attract their wealth because of their purpose in life?

"Nothing splendid has ever been achieved except by those who dared to believe that something inside of them was superior to circumstance."

~ Bruce Barton

Your higher purpose will bring about true lasting wealth. Universal laws work perfectly and harmoniously when an ideal with a higher purpose is your focus. It's as if everything seems to fall into place.

You can use your own experiences as evidence of this fact. Just compare your results in life when your desires and actions were focused on high ideals to the benefit of all versus the times when you had selfish desires or ulterior motives.

We all know people who have fortunes but didn't have to do a thing for them, and we ask, how did this happen? What's their higher purpose? They didn't 'earn' their fortune, and they certainly don't use it for the benefit of a higher ideal.

Keep in mind that this artificial wealth is likely limited or will be lost. You can't have true wealth that is long-lasting if you don't earn it based on an ideal that benefits more than just yourself.

You can see this play out often in business. Most truly successful business people are idealists who continue to strive to be better or for better ways of accomplishing things. They don't allow the current standards to run their businesses, and they run their businesses with high moral and ethical standards to sustain their success.

It's also wise to understand that financial wealth's real value is not in the things you have or the amount of money in your bank account but in spending or exchanging what you have for something different and new, for something that allows your creative spiritual power to take root.

All creation is a result of spiritual power, nothing else, and there are three simple yet complex steps to apply this power: idealization, visualization, and materialization.

Hold the perfect picture in your mind to bring about a different result in your life until your vision has been manifested. Don't worry or give thought to any outer world situations, as they are irrelevant in the perfect idealism within your mind. Just picture the result as you desire it to be without limitations.

It may not be easy to understand how thinking a thing will bring it to occur, but it is a scientific fact that it will manifest. Feel free to bring the 'how' it works into your current belief system any way you desire. The 'how' can be believed that God or Jesus delivers to you what you are worthy of, what you have risen in consciousness to know He will deliver.

Don't be overly concerned about how this works. Be reassured it works. We may never prove in this lifetime how it works. Just have faith, know that it works every time, and allow it to work for you.

Understand that you cannot experience something in your outer world if it isn't a condition you have in your inner world. Therefore, your success depends upon what you can vividly imagine in your mind's eye as an end desired result.

Every experience you have is a result of preceding thought. There are no coincidences in life, just as there's no such thing as being lucky or unlucky. All your circumstances are a result of clearly defined thought.

Thought is what changes your life's perceptions. And perception is your reality. Whatever you experience, everything you say, think, see, and feel becomes an impression and mental image influencing your beliefs. Yet you can also create your mental images without having to have experienced them. Regardless of circumstance, environment, or external sources, your thoughts can be the source of your mental pictures. This ability gives you the power to control your destiny.

It is the application of this power that allows you to determine your fate. When you consciously realize a condition in your mind's eye, that condition will manifest in your life. 'Thinking is the one great cause in life.' Therefore, controlling your thoughts allows you to control your destiny.

Thoughts must be formed precisely as you desire the result. The greater the feeling and love for others within your thoughts, the more vitality they are given. The vitality given by love will affect the speed at which your seed of thought will grow and manifest.

Consider three characteristics of thought: form, quality, and vitality. The form of your thought is one of clarity and boldness of the images you create in your mind's eye. The quality of your thought depends upon the substance. Meaning it depends upon the purpose and how much courage, determination, and vigor your thoughts hold. The amount of feeling within them determines the vitality of your thoughts. The more feeling of love for others in your thoughts, the greater the vitality. This gives thought life and allows it to grow and expand.

Constructive, harmonious thoughts always manifest positive results through the *Laws of Love, Attraction, and Growth*. Destructive thoughts that are not harmonious stick with you, and results follow these destructive thoughts, bringing evil and disease into your life.

Destructive thoughts won't grow outside you. They eventually will die within you and often kill a part of you in the process. Destructive thoughts are often referred to as evil. When we bring evil upon ourselves, it is simply our environment and body acting in equilibrium with our minds. It is neither good nor bad; it simply is. The body follows the mind, and our outer world can only mirror our inner world.

Your devil is your destructive thoughts, and evil is simply a word that describes your actions and outcomes resulting from your disempowering thoughts. Among all things, destructive thought must be eliminated.

The way you are guaranteed success is to focus on constructive thoughts. By visualizing your desire, form a mental picture in your mind's eye. By doing so, you will bring it about.

When you visualize, you are experiencing what already exists in the spiritual world. If you are faithful to your ideal, the visualization will one day appear in your outer world. Visualization is a result of your imagination. By imagining things, you impress upon the mind thoughts that form concepts and ideals, which are the plans from which the Master Architect designs your future.

"Your imagination is your preview of life's coming attractions."

~Albert Einstein

Feeling and thought in combination are irresistible. Some psychologists believe there is only one sense versus five or six. They believe that all senses are just modifications of the one sense of feeling. This supports why loving feelings gives life to thought. It is what gives thought power.

Visualization must be a conscious effort and represent exactly what you desire, versus a subconscious activity in which you realize whatever comes your way or images that represent your current belief system. Actual change in your life will only occur when you consciously direct your thoughts and mental images to the desired picture result.

Don't allow mental images that are not consciously directed and keep focused on your desires. Stay focused on the result – a farsighted vision of perfect resolution.

Meditation Exercise Sixteen

As always, take your position and relax your body and every muscle and nerve. Relax your mind and inhibit thought. Now bring yourself to a realization of the critical fact that harmony and happiness are states of consciousness and do not depend upon physical things.

Things are effects and come because of correct mental states. Therefore, if you desire material possessions of any kind, your chief concern should be to acquire the mental attitude that will bring about the desired result. This mental attitude is brought about by realizing your spiritual nature and your unity with the Infinite, which is the substance of all things. This realization will bring about everything necessary for your complete enjoyment. This is scientific and correct thinking.

When you succeed in bringing about this mental attitude, it is comparatively easy to realize your desire as an already accomplished fact. When you can do this, you will have found the 'truth' that makes you and everyone 'free' from every lack or limitation.

Concentrated Thought

Chapter Seventeen

You've heard the phrase 'man has dominion over all things,' haven't you? As you have learned, you do this through your thoughts. Thought is spiritual and united with the Infinite. Thought is the process that determines your circumstance every time.

You may be used to relying upon your five senses, but it is your 6th sense, your spiritual connection, in which all ideals are conceived. You can quickly obtain intuitive knowledge through a concentrated focus. The vibrations generated by your thought are what assemble the forces that provide the answers to all your questions.

Become conscious that your inner thoughts take hold of your Spirit. The Spirit of a thing is the thing itself. Without the Spirit or soul, the body is dead. The Spirit is a vital part of anything and is the aspect in which we are all connected. Your body is the outward vision of your Spirit, which is the case with all things. Therefore, thoughts focused inwardly speak to the Spirit, the soul of all things, united with everyone and everything. No wonder thoughts are so powerful.

When you consider all power within your control, mental power is superior to all other sources of power.

Most people spend years studying and working with numbers to ensure that they understand mathematics. Similarly, to understand the power of the mind, you will need to study and work with your mind and come to a conscious understanding of the omnipotence of your thoughts.

Your concentrated focus, as with anything, gets stronger with practice over time. Your continuous flow of thought, delivered persistently yet patiently, will provide the strength to plant the seeds that grow.

Think about an actor playing a role in a movie. You begin to understand the true talent of the best actors. They get so engrossed in their roles. They instinctively react and act as if they became the characters versus acting the parts. This is an excellent analogy for the definition of concentration. It is essential for you to become so interested in your thought, so immersed in your subject, that you can't be conscious of being anything else. It's as if you're already living the part.

Decide whom you want to be. Determine the role of the actor. Then play the part with everything you have. Become so immersed in your role that you leave the old you behind.

This level of concentration sets the forces of the Universal Mind in motion to deliver to you what you desire. You become a magnet.

> *"Whatever it is you envision for yourself, no matter how lofty or impossible it may seem to you right now, I encourage you to begin acting as if what you would like to become is already your reality. This is a wonderful way to set into motion the forces that will collaborate with you to make your dreams come true."*
>
> *~ Doctor Wayne Dyer*

When you instinctively begin to act the part, your subconscious mind already believes it to be true. When your subconscious has risen to what you desire, the evidence of your accomplishment will appear.

Concentration requires practice and, most importantly, an ability to control your mental and physical being. One of the keys is to stop focusing on what you want to have and focus on becoming whom you want to be. You cannot get the things you want until you become that person in consciousness.

An exceptional golfer focuses on the ball falling into the cup. Tiger Woods says, "be the ball." The result of this type of thinking is that there is a skill developed in getting the ball in the cup. A CEO of a successful company studies the area of their business and other businesses to envision and deliver a more successful company. Again, thinking in this regard will result in an improvement in the skills required to fulfill the needs of the company.

When we focus on anything other than being who we desire to be, the result is the opposite, and we become the person in the outer world that we are in our inner world.

You may have learned unintentionally to create what you do not want or to be something other than what you desire by thinking disempowering thoughts. Negative thoughts don't work toward achieving what you desire. They work against you.

Focusing on anything other than being the person you want to become will not deliver the desired result. This weakness impedes attaining the desired state of consciousness, and therefore, an impediment to accomplishing what you desire.

It is essential to become in consciousness the person you desire to be. This is accomplished much more quickly when the concentrated focus is mixed with a burning desire. The greater and more constant the desire, the more powerful the result.

When we look at many successful businesses and transactions with them, we find that the mental aspect of the business is the primary controlling factor. In other words, desire is the primary force. Your thoughts are to stay the course and be highly directed. Even in business, we can easily see that relationships and results are simply the externalizations of desire.

All of us are meant for greatness. It's within every one of us. However, the mind must develop the greatness that only can come from within. Your thoughts are what give you omnipotence. Physical effort doesn't come close to delivering the powerful results that your thoughts can deliver, as our thoughts channel all-natural power through our spiritual connection with the Divine.

The vibration created by a concentrated focus of thought connects with and attracts what's necessary to deliver your desires. Refrain from allowing the petty nonessential stuff to bog down your thoughts and impede your desired result.

Your mind must be strengthened to rise above the distractions of the day-to-day business and everyday happenings within your outer world.

There is nothing mysterious about it. When your thoughts are focused and persistent, they become identified with your vision. When you concentrate on a definite purpose, your subconscious will set forces in motion vibrationally to deliver to you the resources needed that will lead to success.

Once you plant the seed of thought, you must be ready for what presents itself to you. The Divine speaks to you intuitively. He reveals the truth you need precisely. It doesn't matter if you have the knowledge or experience that would typically be necessary. Your intuition will lead you to what you need.

Trust your intuition and work with it. Develop and nurture this power within you. Recognize and appreciate your intuition.

If you welcome, appreciate, and are thankful for what your intuition has given you, you will welcome His voice in the future. The more you welcome the insight delivered through your intuition, the more you recognize the gift of what is being presented, the more frequent His calls will become, and the more intuitive gifts you will receive.

Seek solitude frequently, as Divine inspiration usually appears in the silence. You don't need hours, just minutes daily. Step back, take a deep breath, and clear your mind.

Your intuition is a subconscious function, and the subconscious is omnipotent. Through your connection with the Infinite, your subconscious has unlimited resources and unlimited potential and power. However, a lack of desire can restrict and limit your access to these resources. You and your burning desire opens the door to Infinite resources. It is your lack of desire that limits access as well.

Your desire and predominant mental attitude are in direct proportion to the level of success you'll achieve. If you focus on a definite purpose, your subconscious will activate the Eternal Energy to deliver to you the resources needed to attract those things you demand.

The *Law of Love*, expressed through a definite purpose, positively serves others, and we earn happiness by serving others. Obtaining symbols of happiness, wealth, and power will ultimately be lost if they aren't earned by serving others.

You can only receive if you give—those who try to get without giving lose regardless.

Money has always been seen as a symbol of power. However, it should be seen only as the medium to accomplish your goals; it's a resource only. Those who are wealthy don't concern themselves with money. They have learned that money itself is not of importance. The actual importance is your purpose. With a definite purpose that serves others, all resources present themselves.

When your desire is in harmony with natural law, and you become so identified with the object of your thought that you are conscious of nothing else, then the invisible energy begins to be molded, which irresistibly brings you surroundings in correlation with your thought.

Meditation Exercise Seventeen

Relax the mind and body completely. Take the time you need to relax. Now concentrate on becoming in consciousness what you desire. Avoid any thoughts regarding your perception of outer world limitations. Remember that power comes through repose. Let the thought dwell upon your desire. Picture yourself being the person you desire until you completely identify with it and are conscious of nothing else.

If you wish to eliminate fear, concentrate on courage. If you wish to eliminate lack, concentrate on abundance. If you wish to eliminate disease, concentrate on health.

Visualize a situation where you will experience the opposite condition of what you want to be eliminated. See what you're wearing, the venue, the people around you, and your perfect performance. Create a faultless vision. Feel the way it would feel to be this person.

Always concentrate on the ideal as an already existing fact. This is the seed, the life principle that goes forth and creates those causes that guide, direct, and bring about the necessary relations, which eventually manifests in form.

You Are a Vessel for Divine Thought

Chapter Eighteen

Have you noticed the change? You know, the change that's occurring in the world today? Things are changing at the speed of light, or rather, the speed of thought. These changes affect everyone and everything and are beyond compare. As quickly as they are changing now, they will change in the future.

Sometimes we see thought and truth become less of a focus. Faith, vision, and service dwindles, while too many seem more focused on self. However, you can choose. You can choose to ascend in consciousness. So can others and this change can occur just as quickly.

Individually, we are simply the differentiation of the Universal Mind, and who we are and whom we become are brought about by the *Law of Attraction*.

Physical science breaks matter into molecules, molecules into atoms, and atoms into electrons or energy. However, electrons, or energy, appear to be directed by our will or the all-pervading Spirit within us in which we are all united.

All living beings are eternal by the omnipotent power of the Spirit within. The differences in the lives of each of us largely depend upon the level of intelligence we manifest. The greater our understanding and utilization of the Universal Intelligence, the higher scale of being we become or the greater level of success we accomplish.

For example, a dog has a greater level of intelligence and therefore is considered a higher scale of being than a plant. Just as we are a higher scale of being than the dog. The ability to consciously manage our actions and adjust ourselves to our environment is unmatched among all creatures on this earth.

We are created in the image of the Divine and have access to His ultimate power and resources. Our ability to listen to our inner voice, and change direction, when necessary, is crucial to our success in all things, and the Universal Mind responds precisely every time. When we feel something's wrong, that is the Infinite telling us that we are to change course in our direction because our current course or thoughts are off track. We have been given all the intuitive power to communicate with the Divine and adjust our lives and actions according to natural laws.

Natural laws have enabled us to do so many things. The greater our intelligence, the greater our understanding of natural laws, and therefore the greater power we possess because of our ability to recognize and live in alignment with the natural laws. You are simply the individualization of this Universal Intelligence, and the more you understand that the Universal Intelligence permeates everyone and everything, the more you are free, knowing that you have access to this intelligence that is responsive to every demand.

Thought is creative and spiritual. However, all thought does not originate in the individual but in the Universe. You are simply a vessel for Divine thought. The Divine is the source and foundation of your thought, energy, and substance. We are just a vessel for individual expression and creation.

Through thought, we come together with the Divine, where we, as finite beings, unite with the Infinite. Thought is the magic that brings vitality to our physical being and transforms us into one who feels and acts. The Infinite creates through the individual with thought.

Through the *Law of Attraction* that each electron has for every electron, the Divine manifests itself in the physical world. The energy created by thought initiates electrons to come together in form and fulfill the creation of the image in thought.

Everything created is a result of thought attracting and combining electrons into form. This truth has been tested consciously or subconsciously by everyone and continues to prove to be true. This truth's usefulness is directly proportional to your understanding and application of it.

Remember that you are a complete thought entity, meaning you receive only as you give. Growth results from the *Law of Reciprocity*, and like attracts like. The energy produced by thought responds only to the extent of its vibratory harmony.

Therefore, your wealth is seen to be what you inherently are. Affluence in your outer world occurs when you are affluent within. Physical health occurs when you're mentally healthy and happy and being abundantly loved will occur only when you abundantly love others and are filled with love.

> *"Work like you don't need the money. Love like you've never been hurt. Dance like nobody's watching."*
>
> ~Mark Twain Samuel Clemens

When you continually give and give, you will continually be given more.

The unlimited power of the Universal Mind will only work to your benefit if you channel the power through constructive thought. This omnipotent power depends upon you understanding it and applying it.

To fully use this unlimited power, you must cultivate the ability to give proper attention through practice. The more attention you give, the greater your interest becomes. The greater your interest, the more attention you give. One follows the other.

To develop a strong interest in anything, pay attention to it consciously. This practice will enable you to cultivate the power of attention and direct your thoughts to manifest your outer world.

The proper understanding of the *Law of Attraction* is nothing more than believing, which has been put to the test and demonstrated to be a fact. It is our living faith or truth.

Meditation Exercise Eighteen

As always, go to your room and take your position. Completely relax and let go of all stress and negativity. Totally relax. Now concentrate upon your power to create. Seek insight and perception and find a logical basis for your faith.

Let the thought dwell on the fact that we, as physical beings, live and move in the external world with air that we must breathe to live. Then let the thought rest on the fact that we as spiritual beings also live and move within a similar but subtler energy upon which we depend for life, and as in the physical world, no life assumes form until after a seed is sown.

In the spiritual world, no effect can be produced until the seed is sown, and the fruit will depend upon the nature of the seed. The result you secure depends upon your perception of the law in the mighty domain of causation, the highest evolution of human consciousness.

The One Creative Principle of Mental Power

Chapter Nineteen

The search for truth is a sympathetic logical process that allows you to understand the cause behind every effect. Every experience is an effect, and the cause is something you can consciously control. Your experiences are not of chance. They are not of your upbringing or the past. Your experience is of destiny that is appropriately directed by your conscious thoughts.

Ultimately, natural laws govern the physical world. If you understand the causes and effects of natural laws, you will be able to use these laws to the benefit of all because you will understand the effect of every cause every time. The laws of gravity, electricity, steam, and cellular service for example, are natural laws that work every single time.

One of those natural laws is that of polarity. Any condition has extremes that are opposite of each other. In the physical world, there are many contrasts. There are hot and cold, North and South, top and bottom, light and dark, front and back, and many other expressions that we use to compare opposites or extremes.

But the two names used are just different labels to describe a single condition and the extremes of that condition. The two labels are relative and are simply two descriptions of a single condition or entity.

Similarly, words are used in the mental and moral worlds to describe two extremes that explain a single condition—good and evil, intelligence and ignorance, and joy and sorrow.

Evil is the absence of good, ignorance is the absence of intelligence, falsity is the absence of truth, and sorrow is the absence of joy. All the negative extremes represent the absence of the respective positive extreme. The positive extremes have vitality and are full of life. When you take away life and love, you don't have anything other than an adverse condition. But life and love give vitality to thought and allow the seeds you plant to grow.

In all of the examples given, the negative can be destroyed by the positive. Light always destroys darkness, truth destroys false, love destroys hate, and intelligence destroys ignorance.

The empowering, loving force of the Universal Mind has vitality and grows and eventually destroys any negative condition.

Realistically, there is only one creative principle, one law, in the physical world as well as the nonphysical world. That is that of the creative energy of the Universal Mind, or the Eternal Energy in which all things are created.

You are related to this creative principle through your ability to think, and your empowering, loving thoughts plant seeds that begin to grow.

The Divine creates through you, the individual, and creation requires a physical world that is forever changing.

When you look at the world today, the buildings, homes, and cars, and compare them to those in the world 100 years ago, not one of them comes close to resembling those of the past, just as it is likely that not one today will resemble those of 100 years from now.

We can look at the same analogy and relate it to the animal kingdom or the plant world. There again, we'll see the same *Law of Change*.

The *Law of Change* still rules the earth when we consider the inorganic world. Mountains appear where there was once a lake. The great cliffs and Yosemite Valley can be traced back to the glaciers that came before the cliffs.

The only thing that will not change is that change is constant and never-ending. This is the Divine continuing to create all things anew. All matter is a result of thought taking form. The incredible power of the Universal Mind, the Infinite working through everything and everyone, ensures that change and creation are never-ending.

However, the Universal Mind is a pure mind in static form or at rest. Our ability to think is our ability to act upon the Universal Mind and convert it from a static mind to a dynamic one. It is thought that is the energy that brings ideas into manifestation through the power of the Universal Mind. It is as if God waits patiently until we act upon His power through thought. Then, with unconditional love, He uses His unlimited resources to deliver what we demand.

Because the Universal Mind is static, it requires energy to start it in motion. Physical energy is furnished by food and correct thinking. The food you eat is converted into energy, enabling you to think. If you stop eating for a long period of time, you will stop thinking. Then you no longer act upon the Universal. There is consequently no action or reaction between you and the Universe. In other words, no cause and effect exist, and the Universal is only pure mind in static form – a mind at rest.

Ultimately, even spiritual activity doesn't occur in the physical world without using physical things such as food for energy.

However, thought constantly and eternally is taking form and is looking for expression. Therefore, in addition to furnishing our bodies with food, we feed our bodies with empowering, loving, constructive thought. Whether you realize it or not, powerful, constructive, empowering, and positive thoughts will be evident in your health, state of mind, business, and environment because your solar plexus expands, supplying energy to every muscle and nerve and beyond. Your vibrational rate aligns with the Universal Substance, attracting all that is required.

When your thoughts are full of weakness, disempowerment, destructiveness, and negativity, they ultimately manifest as some fear, worry, or nervousness and will also be evident in your health, state of mind, business, and environment. Your solar plexus contracts, paralyzing the muscular system. It affects your entire body. Your vibrational rate is not aligned with the Universe, leaving your disempowering thought with you to rot.

There's a belief that physical possessions represent power that will lead to happiness. Although physical possessions represent power, the power fails to compare to mental power.

But what is this mysterious vital force called mental power? Does anyone know?

We don't know, but neither does anyone know what electricity is. We do know that conforming to the requirements of the law by which electricity is governed, it will give us the electrical power we desire. Similarly, we do know that by conforming to the requirements of the law by which mental power is governed, it, too, will give us the power we desire.

Thought that is forced with a finite purpose that serves others is the vital force that allows the seed of thought to grow. Thought is the vital force or energy that has access to unlimited mental power through our unity with the Infinite.

You likely understand at this juncture that everything is energy and even matter is not solid. Matter is composed of particles held together at a high rate of vibration.

The omnipresent substance or Eternal Energy from which all things are created is infinite in quantity and is universally present.

It's easy to look at how light travels and better understand the Eternal Energy that guides it. Light travels about 186,000 miles per second, and some stars that can be seen are so far away that it takes 2000 years for the light to reach earth.

Yet it travels along in waves through the Omnipresent Substance at unbelievable speed. If this can occur, and it clearly can, then it is evident that this Eternal Energy or Omnipresent Substance is universally present.

So how does this Universal Substance manifest in form? All things in this physical world depend upon the rate of vibration and the resulting relationship of atoms to each other. If we want to change the form of manifestation, we have to change the relationship of the atoms to each other, and we do this by changing the rate of vibration.

How do we change the rate of vibration? By changing our thoughts...

Meditation Exercise Nineteen

You are to concentrate. When you concentrate, do so with all that the word implies. Becomes so absorbed in the object of your thought that you are conscious of nothing else and do this a few minutes every day. Become in consciousness what you desire to be.

Take your position and completely still your body and mind, then relax your body and inhibit all undesirable thought. Concentrate on being the person you desire to be. Let the thought rest on the fact that appearances are deceptive. The earth is not flat or stationary, the sky is not a dome, the sun does not move, the stars are not tiny specks of light, and matter, which was once supposed to be fixed, is in a state of perpetual flux.

Realize that the day is fast approaching when modes of thought and action must be adjusted to rapidly increased knowledge of the operation of external principles.

The Omnipresence of God

Chapter Twenty

God is love, and God is omnipresent. True? Most believe so. If this is true, then there is nowhere that God isn't present, wouldn't you agree?

If God is everywhere, then where are Satan and hell? Where is evil?

Most will also agree that we are made in the image and likeness of God, and therefore we must be spiritual beings. Our ability to think is our ability to create; therefore, thinking is a creative process and the activity of the Spirit. God is the Spirit within us, and the Spirit is the creative principle of the Universe. All form is simply the result of the thinking process.

When the creative power of thought is manifested for the benefit of humanity, we call the result good. But when the creative power of thought is manifested destructively, we call the result evil.

This suggests the basis of both good and evil. They are merely words used to describe the quality of the result of the thinking or creative process.

Let's explore the God within each of us. When you say, 'I want to go over there,' who is 'I'? We already know the 'I' is your Spirit. You are a spiritual being, and the Spirit of you is you. Without your Spirit, you'd be nothing.

You could be the wealthiest person on earth. However, if you don't recognize it and if you don't make use of your wealth, it has no value at all. Similarly, it also has no value if you don't recognize or use the Spirit within you.

Thought is your spiritual power. Until you recognize this, you have no power at all. All great things come through our recognition and use of our resources.

You will achieve only temporary superficial results until you recognize the power of thought and consciousness. The more you recognize the spiritual power of thought, the less physical work will be required, and the more inspired thought you will experience.

The secret of the power of thought and consciousness lies in understanding the principles of your mind and your relationship to the Universal Mind. The principles don't change. They're consistent and reliable. The stability offers you an opportunity because you are the vessel for its activity, and therefore you have the power of creation.

The essence of the Universal is within you. It is you. When you recognize this, you will begin to feel the power. You will begin to act as you have never before. It is what will spark the light to your inspiration. It is what gives vitality to your thought. It is what unites you with the invisible forces of the Universe. It is the power that has no fear and leads you down the path to greatness.

You are an imagination workshop, a visualizing entity; what you visualize in your mind's eye in silence will become your great purpose.

Understanding this principle will allow you to use it whenever you require it. Visualize in your mind repeatedly, and the condition in your mind will materialize. True wisdom is being able to call upon the omnipotent power of the Universal Mind on demand.

But if you learn to recognize this inner world that unites with the Universal Forces, and you realize it not only in yourself but in others, in events, in things, and in circumstances, then you will have found the 'Kingdom of Heaven' within.

The power of thought, when understood, can be incredible because it is the secret of all inspiration and genius. It is the most incredible labor-saving device ever dreamed of if used correctly. If misused, it can create disaster and many hours of work.

Every failure we've experienced is a result of the same principle. The principle is unchangeable. It is reliable and consistent. When we picture lack, limitation, poverty, disease, and discord in our minds, we will be delivered the evidence of our thoughts in the outer world.

If you fear an event or an outcome, you can say, 'The thing I feared most has occurred.' If you think mean or ignorant thoughts, you will attract to yourself the result of those thoughts.

When you understand and recognize that the Universal Substance that unites everything and everyone is the source of all power and is within, you tap the source of Divine inspiration.

Inspired thought is the art of self-realization, the art of becoming a vessel for the flow of Infinite wisdom, the art of ideal visualization, and the art of manifestation.

Understand that the Infinite power of the Spirit is omnipresent and, therefore, in the slightest substance and the infinitely large. It permeates all things, even the space and air we breathe. It is present everywhere at all times.

An understanding of this, intellectually and emotionally, will allow you to tap into this power. Your emotional understanding, however, brings vitality to thought.

Therefore, a total understanding is essential to recognize the power of the Spirit within.

I've mentioned many times that inspiration comes in silence and from within. The muscles and nerves must be relaxed. Every part of the physical being must not hinder your ability to receive the inspiration or wisdom necessary to develop your purpose.

Inspired thought comes through your ability to receive these invisible forces, and this art of receiving gives you ultimate power.

You can live more abundantly every time you breathe if you consciously breathe with that intention. The 'if' is a critical condition. The intention directs the attention, and without the attention, you won't secure your desired result. You will get only what you give attention to. You will be supplied with a result equal to your demand.

To receive a more extensive supply, you must increase your demand. Increase your demand for life, energy, love, and vitality, and you will increase your supply.

'In Him, we live and move and have our being.' 'He' is spirit, and He is love. We breathe His life, love, and spirit every time we breathe. His spirit is the Eternal Energy with which we could not exist for a moment without. It is the life of the solar plexus.

Every time we breathe, we fill our lungs with His spirit and visualize our body with this Eternal Energy, which is life itself. This is how we can make a conscious connection with all life, all wisdom, and all substance.

This breath of life is the Universal Substance, and our conscious unity with it allows us to focus and exercise the power of His creative energy. This creative power comes through thought, and the quality of your thoughts will determine the quality of the resulting condition.

Every time you think, you start a progression of causes that will create a condition and faithful harmony with the quality of the thought. Thought, which is in harmony with the Universal Mind, will result in quality conditions. Thought that is destructive to yourself or others will result in conditions that are destructive to you.

You can use thought constructively or destructively. However, the law will not allow a destructive thought to produce a constructive result or a constructive thought to produce a destructive result. Think constructively and get constructive results. Think destructively and get destructive results.

You are free. Yes, you are free right now. You have a choice to use this incredible creative power as you will. You're in the driver's seat. You make the decision. It is your will. However, you must also be prepared, either way, for the consequences.

This is the danger of free will. Some believe that they can plant a seed of thought of one kind and, by their will, make it grow into the result of another. The idea that you can compel compliance by using your power is destined for failure as it alienates the power of the Universal Mind, which is the same power you are seeking to use.

Imagine the individual attempting to force the Divine. The finite in conflict with the Infinite. This is guaranteed to fail and is as inevitable as our well-being is guaranteed when we work in cooperation with the Divine and all that is good.

Meditation Exercise Twenty

Go into the silence and concentrate on the fact that 'In Him, we live and move and have our being' is literally and scientifically exact. That you are because He is, that if He is omnipresent, He must be in you. If He is, all in all, you must be in Him. He is spirit, and you are made in His image and likeness; the only difference between His spirit and your spirit is one of degree.

When you realize this clearly, you will have found the secret of the creative power of thought. You will have found the origin of both good and evil. You will have found the secret of the incredible power of concentration. It's the solution to every problem, whether physical, financial, or environmental.

The power to think constructively, deeply, and clearly is an acknowledged and deadly enemy to mistakes and blunders, superstitions, unscientific theories, and irrational beliefs.

The Big Thoughts

Chapter Twenty-One

The Universal Mind is unconditional; it's limitless. The more we recognize our unity with the Universal Mind, the more we understand that there are no limitations. The more we recognize no limitations, the more we become free.

As soon as you recognize this unlimited power within you, you begin to create the cultivation of this power, and whatever you recognize to be true always manifests in your physical world.

The Infinite Mind is the source of all things. There's only one, and it is indestructible. You are a passage in which this

Universal Substance is being manifested. Your ability to think is your ability to use the power of the Universal Substance and create in your physical world.

> *"Your only limitations are those you set up in your mind or permit others to set up for you."*

> ~Og Mandino

This is awesome! This means we have no limitations on the quality, quantity, and possibilities available to us. Use the analogy of an electrical wire that is hot or live, which will represent the Universal Mind. Now take any dead electrical wire without current, which represents each individual. All that must happen for the dead wire to have all the power of the live wire is for the dead wire to come in contact with the live wire. Instantly, the dead wire that had nothing now has all the power it needs.

The way you acquire all the power you need to master every situation is to become aware of your unity with the All-Powerful. The more you become aware of your unity with the All-Powerful, the easier it becomes to control your thoughts in a manner that will eliminate every undesirable condition in your physical world.

Big ideas seem to overshadow small ideas, to the point of smothering them and making them irrelevant. This makes it easy for you to instantaneously destroy all small, undesirable, trivial, irritating obstacles. Keep your ideas big. Not only do you eliminate the small stuff that clutters your results, but it brings you in alignment with global thought, which will increase your mental capacity and improve your ability to accomplish things of significance.

The creative power of the Universal Mind has no difficulty handling big projects, as it is just as present and huge as in the small ones. This is one of the secrets to success. Think big thoughts. When you realize the creative power of the Universal Mind, you understand how you can bring about any condition by creating the desirable condition in your mind. Any condition held in consciousness for any time eventually impresses upon the subconscious mind an imprint that the Eternal Energy will surge into your physical world.

This is how you produce desired results. The results are simply the reflection of your predominant thoughts, a mere image of who you are in consciousness, your attitude.

"Life reflects your thoughts back to you."

You have learned that your predominant thoughts make imprints on the subconscious mind. These imprints create predispositions that create character, skill, and purpose. The combination of character, skill, and purpose determines the experiences you will have in life.

The experiences that result are due to the *Law of Attraction*. The experience you hold in your mind's eye, or your inner world, attracts a corresponding experience in your outer world.

Your predominant thought is your mental magnet, and the law is that 'like creates like.' Your mental attitude will attract a corresponding condition in this physical world.

Your mental attitude is your personality and is composed of the thoughts that you have been creating in your mind. Therefore, if you want conditions to change, you change your thoughts. This results in a change in your mental attitude, which changes your personality and everything you experience in life.

This sounds easy, but it can be pretty tricky. Your mental attitude is a mere image of the mental pictures you've been giving your brain. If you don't like what you've been giving your brain, create new pictures through the art of visualization and persist until you become in consciousness what you desire to be.

As soon as you change the pictures in your mind, you will begin to change the pictures representing your environment in your physical world. Hold the perfect picture of your desire in your mind until your picture objectifies in the outer world.

If your desired result requires an attitude or resource that you don't currently have today, that's OK. Build it into your picture. Picture all the essentials. They are a critical part of your picture. Include the appropriate feelings. Feelings combined with thought create the irresistible magnetic power that attracts the things you desire. Your feelings give your pictures life, and your life allows things to grow.

Please don't set your sights low; set them high. Make them big; give them purpose. Seek the highest levels because there is nothing too big for the forces of the Universal Mind.

Now make it a habit. Make new habits that result in correct thinking and break old habits of incorrect thinking. All habits are formed by doing. You do something, then you do it again, and you do it repeatedly, and soon you have a habit. Well, that's also exactly how you break habits. If you stop doing something repeatedly, you will break habits as well. Failing now and then is no reason to quit entirely, as one indiscretion now and then will not be powerful enough to overtake your multiple impressions.

There are only two classes of people. Who are you?

Do you look forward or look back? There is no standing still in this world as it is always progressing. If you aren't progressing, then you're going backward. You are either progressing or digressing, continuing to improve or getting worse; you are moving forward or backward. Which is it for you?

> "We can draw lessons from the past.
> but we cannot live in it."
>
> ~Lyndon B Johnson

Are you going to be creating, or one who prefers precedent to progress? You must decide which one you will be. Are you going to look forward and create in your inner world, or look backward and live your future based on past patterns?

Live to create, be part of a better world, and be happy.

We are in a transition. The old way of thinking must make way for progress. When we realize that God is within and that it is through him that all things are possible, and it is with love that the *Law of Growth* responds, then we can frame laws that consider the liberties and rights of all versus the privileged few.

The real interest of democracy is to recognize the divinity of the human spirit. Recognize that all power comes from within and is a result of our unity with the Divine. Not one of us has any more power than any other, except by our surrender of such power; there is no such thing as the doctrine of Divine election. The Divine has no favorites and makes no exceptions. The Divine delivers in the outer world what correlates to your inner world every time for everyone.

When you understand and realize your unity with the Divine and the power of the Universal Mind, the Universal Principle will work in your favor because you will have found the source of all health, wealth, love, and power.

"All things are possible to him who believes."

~ Mark 9: 23

The only limits you have are those you impose upon yourself, as there are no limits to the creative power of the Universal Mind. Dare to believe. Dare to dream. Think of your ideal as an already accomplished fact. Become it in consciousness. Believe!

Meditation Exercise Twenty-One

Take your position and relax your body and mind, and inhibit all undesirable thought. Then concentrate on the truth. Try to realize that the truth shall make you free. The truth is that nothing can permanently stand in your way of success when you learn to apply scientifically correct thought methods and principles. Realize that you are manifesting in your physical world your natural soul forces. Realize that silence offers an ever-available and almost unlimited opportunity for awakening the highest conception of truth.

Focus in silence. Comprehend the omnipotence itself in absolute silence. Silent thought concentration is the proper method of reaching, awakening, and then expressing the extraordinary potential power of the world within.

Our Healing Powers

Chapter Twenty-Two

Two distinct methods carry on the life processes. First is our intake, our ability to use the food and drink we consume. Nutrients are necessary to construct cells. Second is our ability to discard all the leftovers. Our bodies break down and dispose of waste material.

Food, water, and air are the only things necessary to construct cells. This being the case, you might think it would be simple to prolong life. However, it's more complicated. Waste material must effectively and efficiently be discarded. Waste accumulates and saturates the tissues causing autointoxication, which results in illness. In some cases, this order is local, and in others, it can affect your entire body.

Therefore, the secret to good health is as easy as providing our bodies with the proper nutrients and effectively disposing of all waste. The first is much simpler than the second.

To properly dispose of waste material, we must be able to increase the flow and distribution of vital energy throughout our body, and this can only be done by eliminating thoughts of fear, worry, anxiety, jealousy, hatred, and every other destructive thought, which tend to tear down and destroy the nerves and glands that control the excretion and elimination of poisonous and waste matter.

Consider that what we are today is entirely the result of our past thinking. Our character, environment, ability, and physical condition result from our past thoughts. Applying knowledge is how we can make our future whatever we desire it to be.

If you're overweight or your health is not what you want it to be, let's examine your way of thinking. Remember that every thought leaves an impression in your subconscious mind. Every impression plants a seed of thought that begins to grow, and before you know it, you have a health issue if you have disempowering thoughts. Negativity and destructive thoughts contract the solar plexus, which depletes the amount of energy to all your muscles and nerves.

If your current thoughts are negative, what would grow will be sickness, decay, and failure. The question is, what are you thinking? What are you creating? What is the crop that you're harvesting?

Empowering, constructive thoughts expand the solar plexus, which provides additional energy to the muscles and nerves throughout the body. What is considered by many the most effective way to plant the spiritually empowering seed of thought that grows into a fully energized body is visualization.

I can't say this enough. Visualize in your mind's eye the image of perfect health. Keep it a vivid thought. Hold it in your mind's eye until your consciousness completely accepts it. There have been many miracles, as some would call them, through mental imagery. Thousands have overcome physical illnesses and diseases by this method in a few days and sometimes in just a few minutes.

Every time you have a thought, there is a vibration. All form is a mode of vibration. Therefore, anytime you have a thought, you create a vibration that modifies every atom in the body. Every living cell is affected, and there is a chemical change in every group of living cells. Through the *Law of Vibration*, the mind exercises control over the body.

Everything in the Universe is what it is because of its rate of vibration. If we change the rate of vibration, we change the nature, quality, and form. Everything in the Universe is constantly changing because the rate of vibration is constantly changing. Since thought is also a vibration, we can influence changes in existing vibrations with the vibration of our thoughts.

You already have this power and are using it successfully with every thought. The problem, however, is that we often need to direct this power consciously. It is time to use this power to produce only desirable results intelligently. This is easier than it sounds. You know what feels good, and you know what feels bad, right?

Think about times when you felt excited, courageous, kind or any other feeling that felt good. These empowering thoughts created vibrations that brought about desirable results. Remember when you were filled with envy, hatred, jealousy, or depression. Your feelings didn't feel good. Now remember the result, not the short-term results, but the end result.

In situations where you had empowering thoughts that felt good, the result was likely mental, moral, and physical health. In situations where you had disempowering thoughts that you knew didn't feel right, the result was likely dissension, disagreement, and illness. Understand that this is a universal law. We have this power to control our destiny and co-create with the Divine.

The conscious mind directly results in effects on the body. Think about a time when you told an excellent joke and began to laugh hysterically. Your thought controlled that response and ultimately controlled the muscles of your body. If you didn't think it was funny, you didn't laugh. If you thought it was funny, you laughed. In either case, your conscious thought controlled this physical response.

If a situation occurs that prompts sympathy; your eyes begin to water. Sometimes you can't even control this response. You feel something, and your body instantly responds. Thought controls the glands in your body too.

If someone says something to you that angers you, your face begins to turn red, and your blood pressure rises. Your thoughts have some control over the circulation of your blood.

All these examples are your conscious thought immediately affecting your body's muscles, glands, and blood circulation. Conscious thought caused these effects. Because it's conscious thought, as soon as you change your thought, these effects will dissipate.

But what happens when the subconscious mind controls the body? You cut your finger, and immediately thousands of cells begin working to heal this wound, and within days, your cut is nothing but a minor scar, if that.

You break a bone, and again, your body begins repairing, and within a few weeks, your bone is healed. No procedure on earth can cure the way your subconscious mind can.

What happens if you swallow poison? Your subconscious immediately recognizes a problem, and your body will attempt to get rid of it immediately. Your subconscious mind is always working, and you are a self-healing machine.

All these self-healing examples happen without conscious thought. Our bodies self-heal perfectly if we don't interfere with the healing process. The millions of cells in your body are all intelligent and instinctively immediately begin repairing or correcting any illness or disease.

However, these cells respond to your conscious thoughts as well.[11] Unfortunately, our cells are often paralyzed and become impotent by our thoughts of fear, doubt, and anxiety. They are like an army ready, willing, and able, just waiting for the command to cure. But thoughts of illness paralyze them instead at times.

Our way to perfect health is based on the *Law of Vibration*, controlled by the mind. Treating symptoms, or the external ones, without changing your thoughts will result only in a lack of results. The inner world must change for an illness to be cured.

The cause is always within; therefore, to change the effect, we must change the inner cause by changing our thoughts.

The millions of cells in your body are intelligent and will respond to your direction of thought. Your cells are all creators and will create the configuration you direct through your thoughts. Therefore, when you picture perfect images of health in your mind, the creative energy of your intelligent cells will build a body of perfect health.

Your mental attitude controls the quality of the brain cells. If you have a negative mental attitude, your subconscious mind will transfer this to your body. If you have a positive mental attitude, this also will be transferred to your body. To manifest health and vitality, you must think empowering thoughts, which result in the radiation of energy throughout your body.

Every part of the human body and everything in the Universe results from the rate of vibration. Mental action is a rate of vibration. And a higher rate of vibration controls or destroys a lower rate of vibration.

You can make any physical condition in your body change. You picture the perfect physical body and condition and impress upon your subconscious this vision so deeply that you plant the seed of spiritual thought. This begins to grow and creates high- quality brain cells, and the brain cells' character determines the vibration rate. The higher the quality of the brain cells, the higher the vibration, and a higher vibration destroys a lower vibration. The result is an improved physical condition.

There is practically no limitation on our ability to place ourselves in harmony with natural law, which is omnipotent.

Although it is still seldom spoken of by physicians, it is becoming more and more evident that the mind has power and control over the body. There is no doubt that few are aware of how much they can do for themselves when they are ill or with a disease. We have the power to heal any ailment. Mental therapeutics is something all of us can do. We can bring about healing by calming the mind or prompting feelings of pleasure, hope, faith, and love. By occupying the mind with mental work and diverting our thoughts from illness and disease to anything that brings pleasure and love, we have the omnipotent healing power of the Divine within.

Meditation Exercise Twenty-Two

Relax your mind and body and concentrate on this quote by Alfred Lord Tennyson, "Speak to Him, thou for He hears, and Spirit with Spirit can meet. Closer is he than breathing, and nearer than hands and feet." Then try to realize that when you do speak to Him, you are in touch with omnipotence, the All-Powerful.

Realize that this power is also omnipresent and will quickly destroy any and every form of sickness or suffering and substitute harmony and perfection. Thoughts that align and recognize this unlimited power attract all you need.

Some seem to think that God sends illness and suffering. Recognize that this cannot be so because then every physician, every surgeon, and every nurse is defying the will of God. Of course, this quickly reasons itself into absurdity. Let the thought rest on the fact that until recently, theology has been trying to teach an impossible Creator, a Creator who created beings capable of sinning and then allowing them to be eternally punished for such sins. The outcome of these teachings created fear instead of love, and so, after 2000 years, theology has now redirected these teachings.

Appreciate yourself and all. You are made in the image and likeness of God, and you will more readily appreciate the all- originating mind that forms, upholds, sustains, originates, and creates all there is. All are parts of one stupendous whole, whose body nature is, and God the soul.

Financial Abundance

Chapter Twenty-Three

Success is a journey, not a destination. The joy and fun we receive are in the pursuit of our goals, and the achievement of what we desire rather than the possession itself. It's a continuous journey toward the achievement of predetermined, worthwhile goals. As we achieve our goals, we must determine what we would like to pursue next, and we can quickly determine what's next by keeping an open mind and reaching out for the new.

The first principle of success is service to others. We get what we give. Therefore, it should be a pleasure to be able to give to others. The first principle of financial success is financial service to others. There is no difference when you apply success principles to your finances.

"One of the things I keep learning is that the secret
of being happy is doing things for other people."

~Dick Gregory

To become a money magnet, you must include in your plans how you can assist in the financial well-being of others. The more you help others achieve financial abundance, the more money you will attract. When your thoughts and plans include financial benefits for everyone, you achieve financial success for yourself.

The *Law of Cause and Effect* guarantees that you must receive something in exchange whenever you project anything into the Universe. Therefore, unselfish, optimistic, and constructive thoughts will have a much more significant positive effect than pessimistic, destructive, selfish thoughts.

Money is an essential resource in our physical world, and generous thought, considering the benefits of all involved, is filled with vitality. The *Law of Growth* will ensure that this generosity expands, permeating your physical world.

Selfish thought, considering benefits only to you, will contract, collapse, and ultimately die.

When you recognize the omnipotent power abundant in all things, adjust your thought to know that there is plenty for all, and be of service to others, then you will always attract all that you desire.

The wealthiest people in the world did not get that way because of their ability to influence others to lose money or resources. It is quite the opposite. It is because they helped others earn money. The more you are of service to others, and assist others in acquiring wealth and abundance, the more financial abundance you will attract into your own life.

You must hold the things you desire in consciousness to attract all you desire. When it comes to money, there is no exception. Money consciousness is a state of mind. You must be open to all the abundance the Universe offers and act with faith, courage, and enthusiasm when given the opportunity. This does not mean you act blindly, but when a door is open, and it's clear that it leads to what you desire, you are then to walk briskly, yet vigilantly, through the door.

Poverty consciousness is usually caused by fear. If we concentrate on what we fear, we get what we fear.

It is no accident that a small percentage of the population carries most of the wealth and power. Unfortunately, most people accept past precedents and the ideas of others instead of tapping into their power of creative thought within.

Your will directs concentration. You have the conscious power to decide what to think about. If you concentrate on sorrow, discord, and loss, since thought is creative, this concentration leads to more sorrow, discord, and loss. On the other hand, if you concentrate on joy, success, and gain, the creative power of thought will lead to more joy, success, and gain. This principle can be used in business just as easily as any other desire.

All things that are lasting successes are the result of thought, and you have a direct connection with the Infinite

Mind. The Infinite Mind has unlimited possibilities and fantastic ideas that you can put into practical use.

If you take away human nature, what is left is the understanding of an Infinite Presence and Power, the perfect example of which is consciousness – Spirit. It is no surprise that since we are Spirit, we can harmonize with the Infinite to manifest a minor degree of the All-Powerful.

You draw upon the Infinite supply of your ideas, as the Spirit is the soul of consciousness and the source of all ideas. When you realize the true understanding of your Spirit, you will recognize that its laws of manifestation are the most practical thing you can find and are the fundamental nature of all achievement.

If you can find your direct connection with the Infinite Mind or the Spirit and think of big ideas for serving others, you will find financial success.

In application, you use the creative power of thought to build an idealistic vision of what you desire to manifest. By giving your attention to thought, you develop concentration. You can fill in the details of your idealistic vision or change or improve your idea from time to time, proceeding from the initial idea to the finished detail. This power can be applied to anything, including financial wealth and business.

By giving attention to your thoughts in this manner, you develop concentration, and concentration develops spiritual power. Spiritual power is the most substantial influence in existence.

Some may question whether using spiritual power to manifest financial success is an acceptable behavior. Understand that if the Infinite objected, then it wouldn't work. Only that which is in harmony with the Infinite expands and materializes.

Therefore, the power of Spirit is reasonably practical and is the creative activity behind every beneficial activity. It is the Spirit that easily controls and forms matter. Nothing provides more practical value than our thought, which is united with the power of Spirit. Our spirituality is the only absolutely practical thing there is.

Meditation Exercise Twenty-Three

Relax and clear your mind, then concentrate on the fact that you are not a body with a spirit but a spirit with a body. For this reason, your desires are incapable of any permanent satisfaction in anything that is not spiritual.

Money is, therefore, of no value except to bring about the conditions you desire, which must be harmonious. Harmonious conditions necessitate sufficient supply so that if there appears to be any lack, we should realize that the idea or soul of money is service. As this thought takes form, channels of supply will be opened, and you will have the satisfaction of knowing that spiritual methods are entirely practical.

Leave a 1-Click Review!

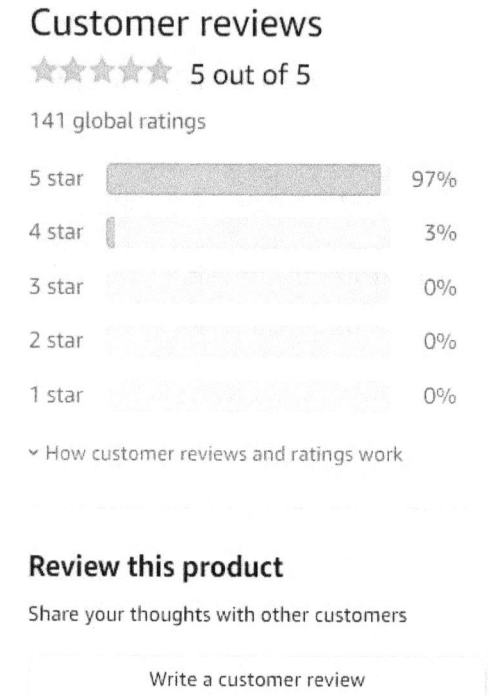

Customer reviews

⭐⭐⭐⭐⭐ 5 out of 5

141 global ratings

5 star		97%
4 star		3%
3 star		0%
2 star		0%
1 star		0%

˅ How customer reviews and ratings work

Review this product

Share your thoughts with other customers

Write a customer review

I would be incredibly thankful if you could take just 60 seconds to write a brief review on Amazon, even if it's just a few sentences.

>> Click here to leave a quick review

The Truth Shall Make You Free

Chapter Twenty-Four

Vibrations are everywhere and amazing. When we hear a noise, it is a vibration that causes a sound to be heard in our minds. We hear sounds that produce vibrations up to 38,000 per second. When the vibration rate exceeds 38,000 per second, we can no longer hear a sound. However, this doesn't mean that there is no sound. It just means that our minds cannot create the sound associated with the vibration.

When we see light, this is also a vibration that, when translated by our eyes, causes light to be seen in our minds. We see light when the vibration rate is at 400 trillion a second. As the vibration rate increases, our eyes translate the vibration into colors.

As the vibration rate drops, our sense of touch translates the vibration as heat.

All these sensations are forms of energy that produce vibrations, and our senses interpret the vibrations as sounds, sites, and feelings. Yet the interpretations occur as sounds, sites, and feelings only in our minds, not in our physical world.

It is clear then that our senses don't tell us the truth about our physical world. If they did, we would believe that the sun moves, and that the world is flat. We must look beyond our five senses to understand the truth.

To have abundance in all things in life, you must know the truth and reverse the evidence of the senses. Reverse the evidence of the senses means that you must think about harmony when there is discord. When there is illness, you must think about health. When there is a lack, you must think of abundance.

Every form of discord, illness, and lack is simply the result of wrong thinking, and correct thinking will correct any undesirable condition that isn't consistent with truth. When you recognize this truth, the truth shall make you free.

Your goal must be to convince yourself of this truth. When you have succeeded in doing so, the truth and your correct thinking will manifest themselves.

The power of your spirit makes this so. Spirit is perfect, strong, powerful, harmonious, and joyous. This truth and thought create the highest rate of vibration there is, and therefore it annihilates every form of incorrect thinking in the same way that light destroys darkness.

The only activity the Spirit within possesses is the power to think; since the Spirit is creative, thought must be creative. When you think the truth, you create what is true; when truth manifests, what is false must cease to exist. Your ability to think is ultimately your ability to use the omnipotent power for the benefit of yourself and others.

When using the word 'God,' most people consider this word to mean something outside of themselves. Yet precisely the opposite is true. It is God or the Spirit within us that is our very life. Without it, we would be dead. As soon as the Spirit leaves the body, the body dies. Therefore, the Spirit is all there is to our living beings.

This truth will enable you to overcome every form of lack, limitation, or illness. The outer world is relative only. The truth is absolute and found only from within us.

It is essential to train your mind to see truth only. Express in your mind true conditions only. The truth is that the spirit or the 'I' within you is perfect, whole, powerful, joyous, and harmonious. It can never have any lack or limitation. Genius and greatness are within us, which come from the Spirit within us—the Spirit, which is one with the Universal Mind.

This truth makes you free, and the conscious knowledge of this truth will allow you to overcome any undesirable condition.

All conditions you experience are created by thought. Therefore, discord, illness, and lack are mental conditions in which you fail to perceive the truth. You must look within and discover the mental error to determine the cause behind any undesirable condition. Your condition will be corrected as soon as you correct your thinking and focus on the truth.

Your physical world will be a mere reflection of your inner world. If you see limitation, lack, imperfection, illness, and destruction, you will experience it. Conversely, if you see abundance, Infinite possibilities, perfection, health, and harmony, you will also experience it.

Everything you are experiencing in your life right now already lives in your subconscious personality, which attracts to it the mental and physical conditions that are agreeable to its personality. Therefore, who you are in your subconscious determines your future, and who you were in your subconscious determined your present.

It doesn't matter what the difficulty is, where it is, or who is affected; you must convince yourself of the truth you desire to see manifest.

The conditions in your outer world result from the conditions in your inner world. Meditation, or prayer if you prefer, when done correctly, will remove any undesirable condition. You must form a mental picture of the condition desired. By holding the perfect ideal in your mind, you can bring about the perfect ideal in your physical world.

Additionally, you can create self-talk or argue against the irrational thoughts that created the undesirable condition, to begin with. Every form of concentration, mental imaging, self-talk, and subliminal auto suggestion is simply a way by which you persuade yourself to realize the truth. However, imagining the desirable condition is the most effective and efficient way to correct any undesirable condition.

Every time you allow your thoughts to rest on any inharmonious condition realize that the condition is only perception and has no reality. Focus on truth.

The Universal Mind in which 'we live and move and have our being' is one and indivisible, and therefore it is possible to help others as to help ourselves. All minds are one mind; this is one of the most challenging concepts to grasp.

To create abundance where there is lack or destroy limitations where there are others involved, you don't need to focus on the others but on driving any belief of lack or limitation out of your mind. The key is clear, decisive, calm, deliberate, and sustained thought with a definite end desirable vision. The result will be accomplished as soon as you have succeeded in doing this.

When you realize this truth, you will have come into possession of the *Master Key*.

You can get out of life precisely what you desire by first putting into life what you desire. The result of this knowledge is the truth that makes us free, not only free from every lack and limitation but free from sorrow and worry. This is the truth that applies to everyone.

If your beliefs are geared toward religion, Jesus, the greatest religious teacher of the world, as well as many other great religious teachers, has shown us the way so clearly for us to follow.

If your beliefs are geared toward physical science, the law will operate with mathematical certainty.

In any regard, understanding this principle is the secret that explains how gold in the mind creates gold in the heart and in the hand. It is the secret that enables you to reach degrees of power that may, to some, seem impossible.

You will also be able to say; it is not I that does the work, but the Father that dwells within me. He does the work. You will understand that the Father is the Universal Mind and that He really and truly dwells within you. You will recognize that the beautiful promise made in the Bible is fact, not fiction, and can be demonstrated by anyone having sufficient understanding. You will know that faith believes this truth.

Meditation Exercise Twenty-Four

For your last exercise, begin as always by taking your position and relaxing your body and mind. Now realize that this is truly a wonderful world in which we live, you are a wonderful being, and many are awakening to a knowledge of the truth. As fast as they awake, they will realize the splendors that exist for those who find themselves in the promised land.

They have crossed the river of judgment and have arrived at the point of discrimination between the true and the false and have found that all they have ever willed or dreamed was but a fragment of the true nature of this dazzling reality.

About the Author

Charles Haanel (b. May 22, 1866; d. November 27, 1949) and Tammy Gallagher (b. March 16, 1964), are technically co-authors. The inspiration of each chapter and their corresponding mediation exercises come from the original *Master Key*. Charles and Tammy's time spent on this earth did not overlap, and they therefore have never had an opportunity to meet. About the only thing the two authors have in common is that they were born in Michigan, were Republicans, and developed the fun interest in the power within.[13]

Haanel, born in Ann Arbor MI, was the son of Hugo and Ameline Haanel.[13] The family moved to Saint Louis when Charles was a child. Charles entered the business world as an office boy for the national enameling and stapling company, for which he worked for 15 years. Haanel resigned his position and organized a company in 1889 that raised sugar and coffee, of which he was made president. The plantation was successful from the beginning and grew to be a company of significant financial worth.

Charles organized the continental commercial company, and ran this business as its president. He was one of the organizers of the Sacramento Valley Improvement company and from the beginning was its president as well.

In 1885, Charles married miss Esther M Smith. 6 years later, Esther's death left Charles a widower with one son and two daughters. Charles remarried, to miss Margaret Nicholson, in 1908.[13]

Although Charles was a republican, his business interests left no time for him to take an active interest in politics beyond voting and using his influence to assist those candidates he supported.

Charles was a member of Keystone Lodge, a 32nd degree Mason, and a Shriner. He was also affiliated with the Missouri Athletic Club.

Haanel could take a calm survey of life and correcting valuing it's opportunities, possibilities, demands, and obligations. He had wisely sought success along the lines of least resistance, and yet when difficulties and obstacles confronted him, he displayed a force of character that enabled him to overcome them and continue on the pathway to prosperity.

Tammy Gallagher, born in Detroit MI, is the daughter of Dominic Cinquemani and Barbara woods. Tammy remained in Michigan with her family through her youth and spent most of her childhood in St Clair Shores, MI. Tammy's father died when she was five years old, and her mother remarried, Warren woods, when Tammy was fifteen.

Tammy began working as a cashier that year at a local fruit market and worked two jobs during college until she decided to quit college and move to Tampa, Florida to become a reservation sales agent with the small commuter airline. Within a year, the company filed for bankruptcy, and

Tammy became a travel agent for a short period of time before she joined Telecredit as a consumer relations representative. Tammy remained with Telecredit, was promoted many times, and ultimately became an outside sales representative. It was here where she remained until the events described in the Introduction.

Life has a way of leading us to our fate, and Tammy Gallagher's life was no exception. She became overweight in her twenties, developed high blood pressure and high cholesterol, and developed Crohn's disease in her late forties. She spent most of her adult life in the residential development industry but found herself leaving the industry in 2018 as she realized she was trading her health for money. She was operating on autopilot and wasn't happy, so she sought to change.

Tammy has learned that 'giving up' is never an option, and she finally returned to college in her fifties to get the degree she wanted. Tammy is a functional nutrition and lifestyle practitioner and author; best yet, she received her health and life back. She now shares the wisdom gained from her experience and education with others as a means of encouragement and support.

In 2018 Tammy decided that she wanted to give back more to the world than she had been able to do by continuing her journey toward mastering a healthy body and mind. She opened Ballantyne Weight Loss Center to help others achieve health as well.

As a businesswoman, Tammy understands that changing one's life requires vision, determination, and perseverance. This book aims to provide people with inspiration and advice on how to reinvent yourself to live a happier, healthier, more fulfilled life.

Other Books You'll Love

https://www.amazon.com/dp/B0BJTJ2HRQ

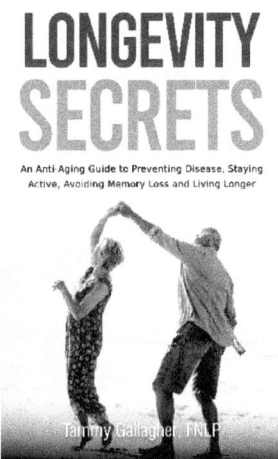

Coming Soon!

Visit https://www.amazon.com/~/e/B0BB8118XK

Get Free eBooks

If you'd like EARLY and FREE ebooks written by Tammy Gallagher or published by TamGall Publishing, sign up here:

tamgall.com/book-reviewers

Just for You!

A FREE GIFT FOR OUR READERS

Get my free eBook on sweeteners...the good, the bad and the ugly. Which sweeteners to avoid and which provide health benefits.

Visit *www.tamgall.com/sweeteners-ebook*

Resources

1. Charles F. Haanel. (2020, June 26). *The History of The Master Key System and Its Influence | Charles F. Haanel.* Charles F. Haanel | the Man Who Unlocked the World, the Author of the Master Key System, and the Father of Personal Development. Retrieved October 12, 2022, from https://www.haanel.com/history-influence/

2. Hopkins, T. (1982, September 29). *The Official Guide to Success, V. 1: Tom Hopkins' Personal Success Program.* Hopkins.

3. Wikipedia contributors. (2022, September 27). *Enteric nervous system.* Wikipedia. Retrieved October 12, 2022,

from
https://en.wikipedia.org/wiki/Enteric_nervous_system

4. Woo, C. (2021, October 15). *Our second brain: More than a gut feeling.* UBC Neuroscience. Retrieved October 12, 2022, from https://neuroscience.ubc.ca/our-second-brain-more-than-a-gut-feeling/

5. Hopkins, T. (1982, September 29). *The Official Guide to Success, V. 1: Tom Hopkins' Personal Success Program.* Hopkins.

6. Abraham, Hicks, J., & Hicks, J. (2004). *Ask and it is Given: Learning to Manifest Your Desires.* Penguin Random House.

7. Vasković, J., MD. (2022, July 6). *Celiac plexus.* Kenhub. Retrieved October 15, 2022, from https://www.kenhub.com/en/library/anatomy/celiac-plexus

8. Kristin. (2022, August 24). *How to Heal & Open Your Solar Plexus Chakra.* Be My Travel Muse. Retrieved October 15, 2022, from https://www.bemytravelmuse.com/solar-plexus-chakra/

9. Bryant, C. (n.d.). *The relationship between attitudes to aging and physical and mental health in older adults* |

International Psychogeriatrics. Cambridge Core. Retrieved October 15, 2022, from https://www.cambridge.org/core/journals/international-psychogeriatrics/article/abs/relationship-between-attitudes-to-aging-and-physical-and-mental-health-in-older-adults/5824A4FC3E98C7DD65F6A4BC0E68E98F

10. *Stress, Anxiety and Your Immune System: How to Avoid Getting Sick | Hartford HealthCare | CT.* (n.d.). Retrieved October 16, 2022, from https://hartfordhealthcare.org/about-us/news-press/news-detail?articleId=18853

11. Cook, G. (2016, January 19). *The Science of Healing Thoughts.* Scientific American. https://www.scientificamerican.com/article/the-science-of-healing-thoughts/

12. O'Connell, C. (2021, April 16). *Quantum physics for the terminally confused.* Cosmos. https://cosmosmagazine.com/science/physics/quantum-physics-for-the-terminally-confused/

13. Charles F. Haanel. (2021, November 24). In *Wikipedia.* https://en.wikipedia.org/wiki/Charles_F._Haanel

www.ingramcontent.com/pod-product-compliance
Lightning Source LLC
Chambersburg PA
CBHW061141120626
46546CB00005B/1879